A GUIDE TO

THE HANDMAID'S TALE

A GUIDE TO

THE HANDMAID'S TALE

PAT LEVY

WITH TONY BUZAN

Hodder & Stoughton

ISBN 0 340 80304 5

First published 2001
Impression number   10 9 8 7 6 5 4 3 2 1
Year   2006 2005 2004 2003 2002 2001

Cover photograph: The Ronald Grant Archive
Mind Maps: Ann Jones

Typeset by Transet Limited, Coventry, England.
Printed in Great Britain for Hodder & Stoughton Educational, a division of
Hodder Headline Plc, 338 Euston Road, London NW1 3BH by Cox and Wyman Ltd,
Reading, Berks.

CONTENTS

REVISION FOR A-LEVEL LITERATURE SUCCESS

You are now in the most important educational stage of your life, and are soon to take English Literature exams that may have a major impact on your future career and goals. As one A-level student put it: 'It's crunch time!'

At this crucial stage of your life the one thing you need even more than subject knowledge is the knowledge of *how* to remember, *how* to read faster, *how* to comprehend, *how* to study, *how* to take notes and *how* to organize your thoughts. You need to know how to *think*; you need a basic introduction on how to use that super bio-computer inside your head – your brain.

The next eight pages contain a goldmine of information on how you can achieve success both at school and in your A-level English Literature exams, as well as in your professional or university career. These eight pages will give you skills that will enable you to be successful in *all* your academic pursuits. You will learn:

◆ How to recall more *while* you are learning.
◆ How to recall more *after* you have finished a class or a study period.
◆ How to use special techniques to improve your memory.
◆ How to use a revolutionary note-taking technique called Mind Maps that will double your memory and help you to write essays and answer exam questions.
◆ How to read everything faster while at the same time improving your comprehension and concentration.
◆ How to zap your revision!

How to understand, improve and master your memory of Literature Guides

Your memory really is like a muscle. Don't exercise it and it will grow weaker; *do* exercise it properly and it will grow incredibly more powerful. There are really only four main things you need to understand about your memory in order to increase its power dramatically:

Recall during learning
– YOU MUST TAKE BREAKS!

When you are studying, your memory can concentrate, understand and recall well for between 20 and 45 minutes at a time. Then it *needs* a break. If you carry on for longer than this without one, your memory starts to break down. If you study for hours non-stop, you will remember only a fraction of what you have been trying to learn, and you will have wasted valuable revision time.

So, ideally, *study for less than an hour*, then take a five- to ten-minute break. During this break listen to music, go for a walk, do some exercise, or just daydream. (Daydreaming is a necessary brain-power booster – geniuses do it regularly.) During the break your brain will be sorting out what it has been learning and you will go back to your study with the new information safely stored and organized in your memory banks. Make *sure* you take breaks at regular intervals as you work through the *Literature Guides*.

Recall after learning
– SURFING THE WAVES OF YOUR MEMORY

What do you think begins to happen to your memory straight *after* you have finished learning something? Does it immediately start forgetting? No! Surprisingly, your brain actually *increases* its power and carries on remembering. For a short time after your study session, your brain integrates the information, making a more complete picture of everything it has just learnt. Only then does the rapid decline in memory begin, as much as 80 per cent of what you have learnt can be forgotten in a day.

However, if you catch the top of the wave of your memory, and briefly review what you have been revising at the correct time, the memory is stamped in far more strongly, and stays at the crest of the wave for a much longer time. To maximize your brain's power to remember, take a few minutes and use a Mind Map to review what you have learnt at the end of a day. Then review it at the end of a week, again at the end of a month, and finally a week before the exams. That way you'll surf-ride your memory wave all the way to your exam, success and beyond!

The memory principle of association

The muscle of your memory becomes stronger when it can **associate** – when it can link things together.

Think about your best friend, and all the things your mind *automatically* links with that person. Think about your favourite hobby, and all the associations your mind has when you think about (remember!) that hobby.

When you are studying, use this memory principle to make associations between the elements in your subjects, and thus to improve both your memory and your chances of success.

The memory principle of imagination

The muscle of your memory will improve significantly if you can produce big images in your mind. Rather than just memorizing the name of a character, imagine that character of the novel or play as if you were a video producer filming that person's life. The same goes for images in poetry.

In *all* your subjects use the **imagination** memory principle.

Throughout this *Literature Guide* you will find special association and imagination techniques (called mnemonics after the Greek goddess Mnemosyne) that will make it much easier for you to remember the topic being discussed. Look out for them!

Your new success formula: Mind Maps®

You have noticed that when people go on holidays, or travel, they take maps. Why? To give them a general picture of where they are going, to help them locate places of special interest and importance, to help them find things more easily, and to help them remember distances and locations, etc.

It is exactly the same with your mind and with study. If you have a 'map of the territory' of what you have to learn, then everything is easier. In learning and study, the Mind Map is that special tool.

As well as helping you with all areas of study, the Mind Map actually *mirrors the way your brain works.* Your Mind Maps can be used for taking notes from your study books, for taking notes in class, for preparing your homework, for presenting your homework, for reviewing your tests, for checking your and your friends' knowledge in any subject, and for *helping you understand anything you learn.* Mind Maps are especially useful in English literature, as they allow you to map out the whole territory of a novel, play or poem, giving you an 'at-a-glance' snapshot of all the key information you need to know.

The Mind Maps in the *Literature Guide* use, throughout, **imagination** and **association**. As such, they automatically strengthen your memory muscle every time you use them. Throughout this guide you will find Mind Maps that summarize the most important areas of the English Literature guide you are studying. Study these Mind Maps, add some colour, personalize them, and then have a go at making your own Mind Maps of the work you are studying – you will remember them far better! Put them on your walls and in your files for a quick and easy review. Mind Maps are fast, efficient, effective and, importantly, *fun* to do!

HOW TO DRAW A MIND MAP

1 Start in the middle of the page with the page turned sideways. This gives your brain more radiant freedom for its thoughts.

2 Always start by drawing a picture or symbol of the novel or its title. Why? Because *a picture is worth a thousand words to your brain.* Try to use at least three colours, as colour helps your memory even more.

3 Let your thoughts flow, and write or draw your ideas on coloured branching lines connected to your central image. The key symbols and words are the headings for your topic.

4 Next, add facts and ideas by drawing more, smaller, branches on to the appropriate main branches, just like a tree.

5 Always print your word clearly on its line. Use only one word per line.

6 To link ideas and thoughts on different branches, use arrows, colours, underlining and boxes.

HOW TO READ A MIND MAP

1 Begin in the centre, the focus of your novel, play or poem.

2 The words/images attached to the centre are like chapter headings; read them next.

3 Always read out from the centre, in every direction (even on the left-hand side, where you will read from right to left, instead of the usual left to right).

USING MIND MAPS

Mind Maps are a versatile tool – use them for taking notes in class or from books, for solving problems, for brainstorming with friends, and for reviewing and revising for exams – their uses are infinite! You will find them invaluable for planning essays for coursework and exams. Number your main branches in the order in which you want to use them and off you go – the main headings for your essay are done and all your ideas are logically organized!

Super speed reading and study

What do you think happens to your comprehension as your reading speed rises? 'It goes down!' Wrong! It seems incredible, but it has been proved – the faster you read, the more you comprehend and remember!

So here are some tips to help you to practise reading faster – you'll cover the ground much more quickly, remember more, *and* have more time for revision and leisure activities!

SUPER SPEED READING

1 First read the whole text (whether it's a lengthy book or an exam paper) very quickly, to give your brain an overall idea of what's ahead and get it working. (It's like sending out a scout to look at the territory you have to cover – it's much easier when you know what to expect!) Then read the text again for more detailed information.
2 Have the text a reasonable distance away from your eyes. In this way your eye/brain system will be able to see more at a glance, and will naturally begin to read faster.
3 Take in groups of words at a time. Rather than reading 'slowly and carefully' read faster, more enthusiastically. Your comprehension will rocket!
4 Take in phrases rather than single words while you read.
5 Use a guide. Your eyes are designed to follow movement, so a thin pencil underneath the lines you are reading, moved smoothly along, will 'pull' your eyes to faster speeds.

HOW TO MAKE STUDY EASY FOR YOUR BRAIN

When you are going somewhere, is it easier to know beforehand where you are going, or not? Obviously it is easier if you *do* know. It is the same for your brain and a book. When you get a new book, there are seven things you can do to help your brain get to 'know the territory' faster:

1 Scan through the whole book in less than 20 minutes, as you would do if you were in a shop thinking whether or not to buy it. This gives your brain *control*.

2 Think about what you already know about the subject.
You'll often find out it's a lot more than you thought. A good
way of doing this is to do a quick Mind Map on *everything
you know* after you have skimmed through it.

3 Ask who, what, why, where, when and how questions about
what is in the book. Questions help your brain 'fish' the
knowledge out.

4 Ask your friends what they know about the subject. This
helps them review the knowledge in their own brains, and
helps your brain get new knowledge about what you are
studying.

5 Have another quick speed read through the book, this time
looking for any diagrams, pictures and illustrations, and also
at the beginnings and ends of chapters. Most information is
contained in the beginnings and ends.

6 If you come across any difficult parts in your book, mark
them and *move on.* Your brain *will* be able to solve the
problems when you come back to them a bit later. Much
like saving the difficult bits of a jigsaw puzzle for later.
When you have finished the book, quickly review it one
more time and then discuss it with friends. This will lodge it
permanently in your memory banks.

7 Build up a Mind Map as you study the book. This helps
your brain to organize and hold (remember!) information as
you study.

Helpful hints for exam revision

◆ To avoid **exam panic** cram at the *start* of your course, not
the end. It takes the same amount of time, so you may as
well use it where it is best placed!

◆ Use Mind Maps throughout your course, and build a Master
Mind Map for each subject – a giant Mind Map that
summarizes everything you know about the subject.

◆ Use memory techniques such as mnemonics (verses or
systems for remembering things like dates and events or
lists).

◆ Get together with one or two friends to revise, compare
Mind Maps, and discuss topics

AND FINALLY ...
◆ *Have fun while you learn* – studies show that those people who enjoy what they are doing understand and remember it more, and generally do better.
◆ *Use your teachers* as resource centres. Ask them for help with specific topics and with more general advice on how you can improve your all-round performance.
◆ *Personalize your* **Literature Revision Guide** by underlining and highlighting, by adding notes and pictures. Allow your brain to have a conversation with it!

Your amazing brain and its amazing cells

Your brain is like a super, *super*, *SUPER* computer. The world's best computers have only a few thousand or hundred thousand computer chips. Your brain has 'computer chips' too, and they are called brain cells. Unlike the computer, you do not have only a few thousand computer chips – the number of brain cells in your head is a *million MILLION*!! This means you are a genius just waiting to discover yourself! All you have to do is learn how to get those brain cells working together, and you'll not only become more smart, you'll have more free time to pursue your other fun activities.

The more you understand your amazing brain the more it will repay and amaze you!

Apply its power to this *Literature Guide*!

(Tony Buzan)

HOW TO USE THIS GUIDE

This guide assumes that you have already read *The Handmaid's Tale*, although you could read 'Context' and 'The story of *The Handmaid's Tale*' first. It is best to use the guide alongside the novel. You could read the 'Characterization' and 'Themes' sections without referring to the novel, but you will get more out of these if you do.

The sections

The 'Commentary' section can be used in a number of ways. One way is to read a chapter of the novel, and then read the relevant commentary. Keep on until you come to a test section, test yourself – then have a break! Alternatively, read the 'Commentary' for a chapter, then read that chapter in the novel, then go back to the 'Commentary'. See what works best for you.

'Critical approaches' sums up the main critical views and interpretations of the novel. Your own response is important, but be aware of these approaches too.

'How to get an "A" in English Literature' gives valuable advice on what to look for in a text, and what skills you need to develop in order to achieve your personal best.

'The exam essay' is a useful 'night before' reminder of how to tackle exam questions, though it will help you more if you also look at it much earlier in the year. 'Model answer and essay plan' gives an example A-grade essay and the Mind Map and plan used to write it.

The questions

Whenever you come across a question in the guide with a star ❶ in front of it, think about it for a moment. You could make a Mini Mind Map or a few notes to focus your mind. There is not usually a 'right' answer to these: it is important for you to develop your own opinions if you want to get an 'A'. The 'Test' sections are designed to take you about 15–20 minutes each – time well spent. Take a short break after each one.

References

Quotations from *The Handmaid's Tale* in this guide are taken from the Virago Press edition.

KEY TO ICONS

A **theme** is an idea explored by an author. Whenever a theme is dealt with in the guide, the appropriate icon is used. This means you can find where a theme is mentioned by flicking through the book. Go on – try it now!

Dystopia

Loss and love

Patriarchy

Freedom and resistance

Violence

Control

 LANGUAGE, STYLE AND STRUCTURE

This heading and icon are used in the 'Commentary' wherever there is a special section on the author's choice of words and imagery, and the overall plot structure.

 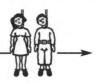

ONTEXT

Margaret Atwood

Born in Ottowa in 1939, Margaret Atwood studied first at
Victoria College in Toronto and later at Harvard. Her early
works were poetry, strongly influenced by myth and fairy
stories. Her early novels were concerned with the conflict
between nature and technology. By the 1970s Atwood was a
prolific writer and had published more books of poetry and
novels. She was also a political cartoonist. She has been an
active member of Amnesty International for many years,
concerning herself with the rights of artists and the treatment
of women in autocratic societies. By the early 1980s she was
publishing feminist criticism and had written children's books
and some television plays. In 1985 *The Handmaid's Tale* won
her both critical and popular acclaim, including the *Los
Angeles Times* prize, a nomination for the Booker Prize and
the Canadian Governor General's award. The novel and the
film also brought several death threats from right-wing
extremists and the work was banned from schools in some
states as being too depressing. Since *The Handmaid's Tale*
Atwood has gone on to become Canada's leading writer and a
feminist icon. Other books to read by Atwood include *The
Edible Woman, Lady Oracle, Cat's Eye* and her latest novel,
The Robber Bride, for which she received the British Booker
prize. She was nominated *Ms* magazine's Woman of the Year
in 1986 and is a Companion of the order of Canada.

The movie

Atwood's novel was made into a movie in 1986 with a
screenplay by Harold Pinter. It forms an interesting comparison
with the novel with its many-layered time frames and the rich
inner life of the heroine. The movie focuses on the events of
Offred's life in Gilead, erasing her memories of her mother,
killing off Luke in the first few minutes and altering Moira's
role in Offred's past life. There are many other changes which

1

radically alter the tone of the novel and the character and voice of the narrator; from the fashionable dress and jewellery of the Aunts and Wives to the imposed exciting ending to Offred's story: Offred murders the Commander and lives happily ever after in a caravan in the mountains. The Commander is made into a despot who abandons Offred and deserves to be stabbed while Serena Joy is quite likeable. The humour of the shabby clothes in Jezebel's is lost and the rich biblical references also disappear. In general the lyrical quality of the novel is abandoned in favour of action.

Try to watch the movie after reading the novel: it seems at times like a summary and there is a fine irony in the fact that the movie has succeeded where Gilead failed – in erasing Offred's past.

The social context

In the early 1980s in the USA there was an anti-feminist backlash. The 1970s had seen great strides in women's rights, increased acceptance of gays and lesbians, and a corresponding fall in the established institutions of the patriarchal state – including marriage, legitimate births and church-going. A religious fundamentalism emerged dedicated to restoring what they called family values. Men such as Jerry Falwell and Howard Philips accused both feminists and the government of 'a satanic attack on the home', and of attempts to 'liberate the wife from the leadership of the husband'. They formed lobby groups aimed at 'every man's right to rule supreme at home', and a man's 'God-given responsibility to lead his family'. This movement is still very much in evidence in the Pro-life (anti-abortion) movement. *The Handmaid's Tale* takes this philosophy and looks at it *reductio ad absurdam* – taken to its logical but absurdly extreme conclusion. When the novel was first published, and after the movie based on the book was released, the book was banned in some schools and Atwood received threats from extreme right-wing groups. Few of the political leaders of such groups criticized it though – they would not have wanted to recognize *The Handmaid's Tale* as being about them or their philosophies.

Atwood has said that there is nothing in *The Handmaid's Tale* that doesn't already exist in some state or another: from the covering of women's bodies in Muslim communities, execution for the 'gender treachery' of being homosexual, or for adultery, to the complete confinement of Afghan women within the home.

The literary context

The Handmaid's Tale exists within the literary tradition of dystopian novels such as George Orwell's *1984*, Burgess's *A Clockwork Orange* and the many feminist novels such as *Woman on the Edge of Time* by Marge Piercy or Ursula Le Guin's *The Dispossessed*. These novels describe a possible future but their main thrust is a critique of the present day and its possible outcome. In *1984* Orwell predicts the massive superstates and their control over every facet of the lives of their citizens while *A Clockwork Orange* looks at the disaffection of youth culture and the failure of modern values. Le Guin considers the massive disparities between the rich and poor and the lack of dialogue of the time between Western capitalist societies and communist communities. Like many women in the 1980s, Atwood looked at the vociferous groups who sought to reverse all the changes that had benefited women through the 1960s and 1970s and issued her form of warning both against their ideas and the separatist ideas of many radical feminists.

THE STORY OF *THE HANDMAID'S TALE*

The story begins some time in the early twenty-first century in Cambridge, Massachusetts. A woman, who we will come to know as Offred, sleeps in a gymnasium patrolled by women with cattle prods. Time passes and she is living in a big house in the same area with a woman called Serena Joy and a Commander. She is their Handmaid; that is, she is a slave whose function is to produce a baby. Her life is restricted to shopping and waiting in her room. She shops with another Handmaid called Ofglen. The town she lives in has roadblocks manned by soldiers called Guardian Angels. We realize that she is living in the USA but there is a new, highly authoritarian government and that virtually all women, not just the Handmaids, have been restricted to the domestic sphere. In a town where once there was a university, bodies of those executed by the state are hung up on a wall. But Offred also has another story to tell which is about her past. Her first memories are about her time at college and her friend Moira. We learn that she has had a daughter taken away from her and has been drugged for a period of time.

Each month Offred goes to a gynaecological clinic, where she is checked. At the clinic a doctor offers to make her pregnant. We realize that Offred has only a limited time in which to conceive before she is sent off to the Colonies – a place for unwanted, sterile or dissident people.

As the story continues we learn more about Offred's past. She was the daughter of a politically active feminist and grew up in the early 1970s in the USA. At college in the 1980s she experienced the first changes in society away from the liberalism of the previous decade. Later she met a married man, Luke, who divorced his wife and married her. They have a child.

When the little girl is about five, a coup takes place in the USA. This follows some nuclear accidents and a period of falling birth-rates caused by pollution and changing attitudes to childbearing on the part of women. The coup robs women of all their rights and gradually the state becomes harsher, attacking first any kind of deviancy from monogamous Christianity and then the various Christian sects. Arrested women have the choice of joining the colonies or, if they are fertile, becoming Handmaids. Some older women (it isn't clear by what process) become Marthas, servants in the houses of the higher echelons of the state, now named Gilead.

Offred's family have been designated enemies of the state because of her husband Luke's divorce, and so the family attempt an escape to Canada. Caught in the process Luke is probably gunned down and the daughter taken away and adopted by a Commander's family. Offred is sent to the Rachel and Leah Centre, where she is indoctrinated into becoming a Handmaid. Offred's mother has disappeared and we discover later in the novel that she was sent to the Colonies. Offred's friend Moira escapes from the Rachel and Leah Centre (called the Red Centre by the Handmaids) and is caught, eventually becoming a prostitute in a brothel run for the Commanders.

Offred attends a birthing ceremony where another of the Handmaids, Ofwarren (Janine), gives birth to a baby which is taken away immediately and given to the wife of Ofwarren's Commander. Offred, like all the Handmaids, takes part in a monthly ceremony where she has sex with her Commander. After one such ceremony, he begins a relationship with her in which they spend time together playing Scrabble, reading and talking. Eventually he takes her to the brothel where she meets Moira. While there, Offred and the Commander have illicit sex.

Serena Joy, the Commander's wife, suggests to Offred that she have sex with the chauffeur Nick, in order to become pregnant. Offred begins a passionate affair with Nick. Her shopping companion identifies herself to Offred as a member of an underground movement called Mayday. One day after a Salvaging – an event where dissidents are hanged, and in one case torn to pieces by the Handmaids – Ofglen commits suicide rather than be arrested. Serena Joy finds out that Offred is seeing the Commander, and the now pregnant Offred is taken away by the secret police, or possibly a group of dissidents within the secret police. We hear no more about Offred, and the story ends a hundred or so years later, long after Gilead has ceased to exist, at a conference which discusses her story, unearthed as a collection of audiotapes some distance north of Cambridge, Massachusetts.

C HARACTERIZATION

The Mini Mind Map above indicates the main characters in *The Handmaid's Tale*. When you have read this section look at the full Mind Map on page 17 and then make a copy of the Mini Mind Map and try to add to it from memory.

In some ways characterization takes second place to the exposition of a set of ideas in this novel. Offred is a fully rounded character with a strong inner life but others are more shady figures, almost stereotypes at times – Moira the radical lesbian feminist, Janine the classic victim, Serena Joy, the castrating bitch. We have no access to their inner thoughts or motivations and view them through Offred's eyes. On occasion she attempts to speak for them, as when she tells the story of Moira's escape. Much of this novel is about how the state reduces individuals to a mere function. Ofglen is replaced in body while the name and the function remain. Offred herself tries to merge Luke and Nick but finds herself unable to do so.

> **Offred:** *Real name not known; the recording voice of the narrative*

A victim of the harsh regime set up in an imaginary future in the USA, Offred has lost everything that once defined her –

her name, her job, her husband, child, mother, friends, possessions. She lives in an unwanted part of someone's house, given things to do in order to keep her fit to bear children, and her only function is the monthly ceremony. The only variations in her life are the Prayvaganzas, Salvagings and births.

In order to survive under these conditions Offred has developed a kind of multiple vision. She lives and relives moments from her past life which superimpose themselves on whatever she is doing at the time. In the first chapter of the book Offred uses the image of a palimpsest, a medieval manuscript which has been scraped clean and reused but where the earlier material is still visible through the later writing. To Offred, Gilead is a palimpsest. She can see her past life and uses it to judge the present and to give her some hope. If she retains her sense of the past, perhaps there will be some future for her. This manifests in different ways. We have, for example, her reveries while she is alone in her room remembering her family, but there are also moments such as the one where she sees the front lawns of the big houses and recalls herself and Luke looking over them.

If Offred has now lost everything that once defined her she does not give in to the system which has made her a woman of reduced circumstances. She lacks the bravura or political awareness of Moira or her mother. However, she maintains her memories and her ability to judge as an act of rebellion against the state. Several of her partly recalled memories are to do with television programmes about the Nazi Holocaust and, like the survivors of that terrible event, she bears witness in her story to the suffering of the innocent victims of this state.

What defines and maintains Offred's sense of identity is her wicked sense of humour. Even as she accepts her undignified status as a Handmaid she can tease the guards at the roadblocks, aware that all she has is *the power of a dog bone – passive but there*. After the terrifying first meeting with the Commander, which turns out to consist largely of a game of Scrabble, she is able to burst out laughing at the foolishness of her situation.

She is a desperately lonely person, having no one with whom to share her sense of outrage and loss. She notices every nuance of the Marthas' attitudes to her and wishes only for a little human companionship. Serena Joy is lost as a possible friend from her first meeting with Offred and later, when they enter a conspiracy together to get Offred pregnant, Offred learns just how unpleasant this woman is – she knows about Offred's daughter and has never mentioned it. Ofglen offers a form of relationship in the almost foolish Mayday organization, but by that time Offred has made a life for herself and has abandoned her past. She has never even found out Ofglen's real name.

Ironically the only relationship of any depth that Offred develops is with the man who is most responsible for her situation – the Commander. But even this is a sham. He wants her to kiss him as if she means it but gives no thought to what he has perpetrated against her and other women. They flirt in the old-fashioned way, Offred always aware that one false move could end her life. Symbolic of this pretence that the old days can still exist for a few high-status men is the trip to Jezebel's with the shabby clothes and the Commander's pleasure in recounting what powerful people some of these slave prostitutes once were.

There is a sense in which Offred is reconstructing herself in this novel. In the early chapters she is a blank figure with no name, and shattered, incomprehensible memories. Her progress through this narrative depicts the way in which she reconstructs what she used to be as her flashbacks finally come together to make sense of her past. It also shows how she makes a new place for herself, accepting the room she sleeps in as her own space and carving out an existence for herself, however humble and restricted that is and eventually saying goodbye to the figures from her past as she forms a new relationship with Nick.

In the debate about feminism which takes place in this novel Offred represents the complexities of modern post-feminists who have moved beyond the binary oppositions of Offred's mother (man–bad, woman–good) or even Moira, to recognize the complexities of gender relations.

The Commander: *A bureaucrat who cynically maintains the system while enjoying the pleasures it has put an end to*

Probably Frederick Waterford, formerly in market research, the Commander is a complex figure. He is fatherly, mild and benign, yet he is also a monster who has helped to create this fascist state and hypocritically enjoys many of the sexual practices which it forbids. We never see him in his official role in Gilead and like Offred, have to keep reminding ourselves of his crimes against humanity as we see him try to make Offred's life a little easier. His motives for putting Offred in danger by bringing her to his room are not clear. Perhaps he is a lonely man who realizes that the state he has created is destructive and just wants some reassurance from a pretty young women. Offred herself realizes the banality of her situation when the Commander almost says the time-honoured words that his wife doesn't understand him, *She wouldn't understand. Anyway, she won't talk to me much any more. We don't seem to have much in common these days* (Chapter 25). The Commander is an anachronism. He believes that women suffered under the old freedom, altering their bodies to make themselves attractive, suffering the indignities of bad husbands or worse, no husband. Women, he believes, add one and one and one and one and don't make four. They just see four separate ones, and perhaps, Offred thinks, he is right (page 201).

Offred sees individuals; she cannot merge Luke and Nick. The Commander sees generalizations, functions. To him, one Offred is much the same as another. We watch him engage in the old sexual politics, fishing for compliments from Offred, offering little treats as if he were a father figure and showing off his authority at Jezebel's. He wants Offred to like him and understand his motives and seems quite regretful that in order to create his idea of a perfect society some people should have got hurt. He seems to believe that he is above the laws which he has helped to create and at Jezebel's in particular is asserting his superiority over the state, at the same time controlling it and subverting it for his own pleasure. At the end of Offred's story he seems a pathetic figure; she looks down on him and feels sorry for him. He makes a feeble attempt to prevent them taking her but we know he is a beaten man.

Serena Joy: *One of the elite Wives, bitter and angry at her husband and the state*

Crippled with arthritis, bitter at the loss of her former worth, jealous of her husband and the new system of Handmaids, Serena Joy seems to want a child badly, even to the point of risking her own and Offred's life to get it. She has no sympathy for Offred's situation and bitterly resents her own, reduced to power over her own little regime, where even the flowers in the garden flourish regardless of what she does to them. In this novel Offred plays often with the idea of doubles: she and Ofglen form a pair, and she sees the previous Offred as her twin. There is a similar pairing between herself and Serena Joy, one in blue and one in red. They both depend on the kindness of the Commander, they both want a child (though for very different reasons), they have both lost their former motivation and freedom. The two conspire together to produce the baby they both need. Later in the novel Serena Joy becomes the betrayed, conventional wife, uttering conventional clichés (*Bitch ... after all he has done for you*) when she discovers the purple dress and her own cloak. Offred, for her part, feels guilty about what she has done to Serena.

The most powerful images of Serena Joy are those in her garden where she takes out her anger and frustration on the tulips, viciously slashing their heads off in a symbolic display of her feelings towards Offred. At other times Offred pictures her as a parody of the Virgin Mary. We know also that her real name is Pam. To Offred 'Serena Joy' sounds like *something you'd put on your hair, in the other time, the time before, to straighten it.*

Serena Joy is another voice in Atwood's debate about feminism and women's roles. She is capable of viciousness to equal any man, putting paid to the feminist standpoint of Offred's mother that it was just men who should be avoided.

Moira: *Radical feminist of Offred's generation who fights the system*

Moira is a radical feminist of the 1980s who either opted to become a lesbian or discovered her true sexual orientation after becoming a radical. Long before the coup that generates Gilead she is aware of sexual politics and is far better prepared than Offred when the coup begins. But even she has no idea of just how successfully the men who organized the revolution would be at singling out and destroying dissident groups. She never folds under the pressure of the Rachel and Leah Centre and makes two escape attempts, one of which is partly successful. Her bravery is rewarded with crippling brutality and she ends up in a state-run brothel. Her sense of the ridiculous and her humour are a weapon she uses against the state, and it is her advice that Offred follows when she mocks her own oppressors. Even Moira's final appearance, dressed in a tatty bunny girl outfit at Jezebel's, mocks the men who control her. But she is beaten by the system and her final words are about indifference and acceptance of her fate.

Moira features in Atwood's discussion with the reader about what constitutes bravery and the nature of feminism. She is the 1980s version of Offred's mother – more separatist and radical than the older women in some ways, she chooses sterilization long before Gilead ever comes about. She also takes the rejection of men to its logical extreme of lesbianism. She is admired by all the other women at the Rachel and Leah Centre, showing that the Aunts are vulnerable and that the system can be challenged. But she, like Offred's mother, is finally beaten by the system while Offred, less brave but with the ability to feel sympathy for the people who have harmed her and the drive to survive whatever happens, finds some way out of Gilead. In the contrast between Offred and Moira, Atwood is suggesting that there are many forms of bravery and that just surviving in order to bear witness constitutes as much an act of bravery as does Moira's bravura.

Offred's mother: *1960s radical feminist*

By the time that Offred's Gilead story is taking place her mother is probably dead, having been sent to the Colonies very early on in the Gilead regime. She was an early feminist during the 1960s, when women were fighting for such basic rights as sexual freedom, the right to control their own fertility, the right to terminate a pregnancy, economic equality with men and equality of opportunity in the work place. She is a feisty, dungaree-wearing, independent woman who has rejected all the trappings of femininity – dedication to housework, a sexually alluring appearance, a male companion – but she has failed in her attempts to convince her own daughter that she should be the same. She is aware that her daughter has accepted all the things that the feminists fought for, but still chooses to make a conventional marriage, even playing for a time the role of the other woman in a family break-up.

Offred's mother appears to us in a series of cameos – burning pornography, bleeding after a pro-abortion demonstration, and bickering with Luke. Later she is seen in film footage, carrying a banner in a pro-abortion march and then sweeping up somewhere in the Colonies. Like most teenagers, Offred is embarrassed by her mother's peculiarities, and her memories of her mother are ambiguous – although now, in Gilead, she would give anything to have her mother back, quirkiness and all. She continues her life-long debate with her mother, pointing out in Chapter 21 the irony of the fact that now she, Offred, lives in a women's culture, though not one her mother had wanted.

Aunt Lydia: *One of the few women who believes in and profits from the system*

Lydia is the voice of the women who have betrayed their kind for a grab at power. She has no redeeming features – in some ways we can at least feel sorry for Serena Joy in her reduced circumstances. Lydia is pure villain, manipulative, cruel, *in love with either/or,* that is only able to see simple alternatives. She is the voice of the state, and appears in Offred's brief memories of her words, a series of platitudes and misquotes from the Bible all intended to reinforce the authority of the state: *freedom to and freedom from, modesty is invisibility, ordinary ... is what you are used to, the future is in your hands.* Her character is reflected in her physical description: she has the long yellow teeth of a dead rodent, steel-rimmed spectacles and watery eyes.

Lydia fights for the 'rights' of the Handmaids because it enhances her own power, and she despises the Wives, her natural enemies: *You must realize they are defeated women. They have been unable ... .* Perhaps Aunt Lydia believes in what the state is doing to these women. Later on in the novel she appears in the real time of the story at the Salvaging, at which we feel all Offred's hatred, which is first aimed at Lydia but then displaced by Lydia's own words and directed towards the Guardian accused of rape.

Nick: *The chauffeur and source of Offred's escape*

Far more than the other characters, Nick appears to us through the mediation of Offred. He is a very ambiguous figure, almost pimp-like at times as he arranges the Commander's assignations with Offred, and later agrees to service Offred for Serena Joy. He appears at first as a stereotype, wide-boy chauffeur, winking and nodding at Offred, irreverently half-dressed as he cleans the car, smoking a black-market cigarette, playing footsie with Offred at the Ceremony. For all his cocky poses, he too is restricted to obeying orders and on the lookout for ways to make his life easier. But there is a second Nick who meets Offred by surprise in the dark in Serena Joy's sitting room and who becomes Offred's secret lover.

It is interesting that Offred chooses to report three different versions of their first sexual encounter as if she, or perhaps Atwood, needs to keep Nick's real character a secret from us. In the end we think that Nick might have rescued Offred but that is never confirmed. He may well have been an Eye, as

Offred originally suspected, testing both her and the Commander. Within the novel's debate about feminism Nick is an even more ambiguous figure. He is at once Offred's salvation and entrapment. Through him she finds love and meaningful existence, as well as becoming pregnant, thus sparing her life. At the same time he keeps her from thoughts of escape, makes her reject the Mayday organization's request for information, and keeps her passive in unpleasant circumstances.

Janine: *Classic victim who has suffered in previous regime as well as the Gilead regime*

Janine is the classic victim. Offred both pities her and despises her. In her previous life Janine had been gang-raped and had had an abortion as a result at age 14. Offred recounts her memory of Janine's repeated confessions at the Rachel and Leah Centre and her own disgust at the pathetic state of the other woman. Janine teeters on the verge of a breakdown even at the centre and both Moira and Offred help her to keep an appearance of sanity. She becomes the Aunts' favourite, sharing their information and passing on whatever information she can back to them. When she is posted, Janine the victim is the only one of the Handmaids that we ever see pregnant. Even in her pride at conceiving she is still a victim, abandoned immediately after the birth and her baby condemned to be a shredder. She finally cracks completely at the Salvaging, wandering about with a handful of bloody hair.

Luke: *Offred's husband; like other men at first he benefits from the system and does nothing to stop it*

Killed off in the first few minutes of the movie, Luke is a far more substantial and important figure in the novel. Like Offred's mother we see him in a series of cameos, but these are much more fragmented. First he appears as a lover, then as part of a happy family. Then as the Gilead regime begins to impose itself on their lives, we see him trying to be as supportive as he can to his wife, who is now utterly dependent on him. Finally, when the state poses a direct threat, we see him making an escape bid with his wife and child. Because Offred doesn't know if he is alive or dead his memory keeps her in the past and prevents her from moving on with her life, such as it is. She constantly revises a series of imaginary scenarios in which he is tortured or part of a resistance movement.

Different critics have seen Luke in different ways. In many ways he is a 'new man' – cooking, taking on his share of childcare, supporting his wife when she loses her job and all her rights. In other ways he can be seen as the kind of man Moira would despise. He begins an extra-marital affair. When the state of Gilead is created he does nothing to alter Offred's condition, only attempting to leave when his own security is threatened. Even Offred is afraid that he might be enjoying the power over her that the new state has given him: *he doesn't mind this, I thought. He doesn't mind it at all. Maybe he even likes it. We are not each other's any more. Instead, I am his.*

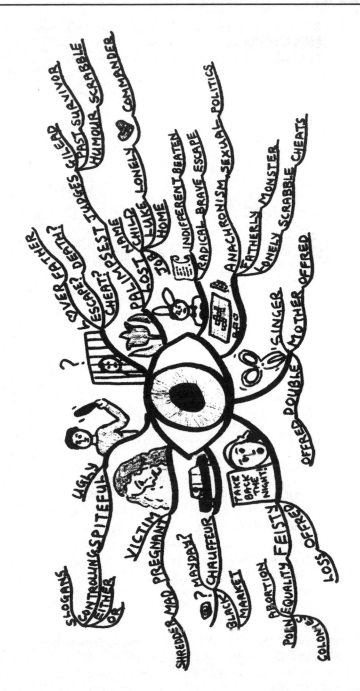

17

A theme is an idea that runs through a work and that is explored and developed along the way. The Mini Mind Map above shows the main themes of *The Handmaid's Tale*. Test yourself by copying it, adding to it and then comparing your results with the version on page 25.

The themes listed below present one way of looking at the novel, but others have been identified. Critics have discussed it in terms of missing persons – Offred herself, her mother, Luke, Moira, Janine, Offred's child. The nature of storytelling itself could also be considered a theme of the novel. Offred regularly considers the nature of what she is doing, and there are scenes that deliberately subvert the idea of a story – such as the love scene with Nick. Moreover, the tale itself is interpreted and judged by the stories which surround it in the epigraphs and the historical notes. The novel also discusses the nature of feminism and women in its various portraits of women and in speeches given by Lydia and the Commander about what was wrong with the old society.

Dystopia

A dystopia is a vision of a society gone wrong. Dystopias are societies where ideology has taken precedence over the well-being of the people within that society, or at least of a sizeable minority. There are, as the Commander says, always some people for whom change is not an improvement. Gilead is one such dystopia, but in order for it to have any significance to us as readers, or for Atwood to want to write about it, the warning that it represents to our own society is equally important.

Written in the 1980s by a Canadian and set in the USA, this novel is a dire warning of the consequences of several things which Atwood saw happening in the USA. What she saw was a backlash coming from right-wing groups and, in the USA in particular, from fundamentalist Christian groups against women's achievements and against the progress made towards equality by the gay rights movement. Modern feminists and representatives of minority groups might say that the backlash is now over and that *The Handmaid's Tale* is no longer relevant. ✪ What do you think? Is there still a threat to equality in our society?

The dystopia that Atwood describes is set very definitely in the USA, in Cambridge, Massachusetts, where Harvard University stands today. It would be recognizable to most Americans. Gilead, named after a biblical place with a very ambiguous history, is a state which is founded on Puritan, Old Testament ethics, and run using modern technology and advertising techniques. In this society most women have been reduced to figures within the home either as Wives or Marthas (servants) or Handmaids. Men also live highly regimented lives, gaining a Wife or a Handmaid only as a reward for good service.

All sexual activity outside of state-sanctioned marriage or slavery is illegal and punishable by death. All religious deviation is also illegal, and nonconformist religious groups who refuse to recant are sent to the polluted Colonies. Black people have been ethnically cleansed to a far distant part of Gilead and the state claims that Jews have been allowed to leave. The state is much smaller than the USA as we know it, and is involved in an ongoing civil war.

This state has come about because of a period of rapidly falling white birth rates and dissatisfaction on the part of powerful men who have seen their power-base undermined both in politics and at home.

Atwood presents this dystopia in the form of a detective story. Aspects of the state are revealed to us in a series of glimpses. At first we see only the surface of the state, its slogans and outward functioning. As Offred settles into her new life, however, we become aware of the corruption and lies. We are eventually shown the extent of the state's cruelty and corruption in the Particicution ceremony, in which a Mayday operative is accused of rape and torn to pieces, and at Jezebel's, where the utter hypocrisy of the men who run the state is revealed. We realize that the biblical propaganda is just a cynical means of control which does not represent the beliefs of the men in power.

Patriarchy

This dystopia takes the statement 'a woman's place is in the home' to its logical misogynist extreme. In Gilead women have been for the most part confined to the home and those that refuse to stay there are destroyed. Women have become identical, replaceable, silent objects. They are classified according to function – Wives, Handmaids, Marthas, Econowives, Aunts, all roles which are geared to the service of the patriarchal state. Offred is not just a slave within this society; she is no longer a human adult. She is like a doll in her responses to Serena Joy, in the way she moves like clockwork with Ofglen; she is like a child in that she is fed childish food, already cut up for her, must not be told unpalatable truths such as what happened to the previous Offred, and must not be allowed dangerous things such as blades or matches. She is a *two legged womb*, useful only for one purpose.

In Gilead, as in all patriarchies, the structure is not a simple one of men wielding power over women. There is also a strict hierarchy among men. The hierarchy is defined in terms of access to the symbols of power – a Wife first of all, whether she be an Econowife or the wife of a Commander, Marthas, a Handmaid for the very powerful and for the highest echelons of all access to a harem of slave women and all the sexual diversions they can offer. Gay men suffer death if they are discovered, doctors who have carried out abortions or had sex with a Handmaid are executed, and male religious leaders are killed or sent to the colonies. The state rewards men who adhere to its rules and punishes those that disobey them. Men can work hard and become more powerful within the system, unlike women, who have become mere chattels.

But if Gilead is a patriarchal culture taken to its extreme, the society that Offred remembers from before also had its faults. Offred recalls stories of rapes and mutilations, and remembers that it wasn't safe to go jogging at night, answer the door even to a policeman, stop to help someone in difficulties on the highway or to leave doors and windows unlocked. She remembers pornography with its undercurrent of male violence against women as well as the preachings even then of women like Serena Joy. The Commander points out the lengths to which women went to find husbands and the abandonment and poverty of some women and children.

The final comment on the patriarchal state comes from the Historical Notes. Gilead is long gone but male sexual jokes have survived the Caucasian dominance of the world, as Professor Pieixoto makes feeble jokes about the pun on the word Tale, or the naming of the women's escape route a 'frailroad'. He denies the importance of Offred's story except as evidence about who the men were who ran Gilead and refuses to pass judgement on the state that abused its citizens so badly. In being blinded by his own cultural attitudes to women, Pieixoto continues Atwood's picture of the 1980s as a misogynistic and discriminatory culture.

Violence

In many ways this novel follows the lines of a modern-day Gothic novel. In the popular Victorian genre an innocent young girl is led along a path of difficulty and hardship, often threatened by being drawn into sexual impropriety, but is rescued at the end of the novel by her beliefs and by the intervention of a handsome young man. The parallels are obvious: Offred is apparently 'rescued' by Nick and Mayday. But this is a modern Gothic novel and underlying it is a much more clearly described, almost sado-masochistic, state-sanctioned violence. Moreover, the rescue itself is ambiguous: we cannot be sure of what happens to Offred, and our uncertainty is shared by the academics who later examine her case.

The violence of this state is evident everywhere in the war conducted against dissidents, the descriptions of rooting out non-conformist groups and Moira's tales of attempted escape. But the really insidious violence in this story is the state-sanctioned violence against people who dare to oppose the state, from the vicious beatings of women caught misbehaving in the Rachel and Leah Centre, to the hanging of corpses on the Wall and the Particicution ceremony. In Offred's life there is the understated violence of the monthly Ceremony. In a parody of Gothic-style suspense, Atwood makes us wait, through sixteen chapters of hints and suggestions, to witness this banal and ugly little scene which disgusts both female participants. We get the impression that the men who run this state do so not out of a desire to increase the population or to create a more moral society, but out of pleasure in the power which they wield.

Atwood, however, is no didact – if the men in this novel are violent so are the women. Serena Joy keeps the knowledge of her daughter from Offred. The Aunts are every bit as vicious as the men in the pornographic movies they show, and the Handmaids themselves, even Offred, take part in the Particicution.

Loss and love

When the Commander asks Offred what she thinks he and his fellow conspirators have left out of the equation, she tells him he has forgotten love. The new state concerns itself with function and denies its citizens the right to love one another. Offred's story is about her love for her mother, husband, child, friend and the difficult nature of that love at times. She is driven through her story by her feelings of loss for her family and for her former life, and the need she has to love at least something.

Offred eventually finds someone to love, but like much else in this story this is ambiguous. Even Offred finds it hard to believe that she should have found love in Gilead and in many ways it is this newly found love that betrays her. She abandons her past and puts all her thoughts into the present and so puts at risk her ability to survive. The passages concerned with her feelings for Nick sound almost like a traditional love story, with Offred describing herself dreamy and smiling at nothing. Her love story terminates rather than concludes as she gives herself up to trusting this man about whom she knows so little.

Freedom and resistance

Freedom – from or to – is one of the motifs of this novel. Gilead has provided its women with freedom from the unpleasant nature of Western society but at the same time it has taken away all their rights. On a personal level the only freedom that Offred has is her freedom to re-enter and re-examine her past and it becomes a form of resistance for her. Within the confines of her room, Offred is able to move about in time. She resists Gilead not in the way that Moira or the Mayday organization can – she is unable to act even when she knows she has been discovered – but by constantly reminding herself of who she used to be and by mocking the state and its institutions.

Towards the end of Offred's story her love for Nick becomes a form of resistance and an area of freedom for her. For the previous Offred, and for our Offred, suicide was and is a constant temptation because it too would be a form of freedom from the state and resistance to it. Offred continually considers suicide and the previous Offred appears in the room with her towards the end, telling her to get on with it. But the option of suicide as a means of escape is lost in Offred's inaction and she leaves with the Eyes not knowing what will happen to her.

Control

The state of Gilead is really all about who can do what to whom, and control is another aspect of the patriarchal state. The Commander controls his household with a light touch – they anticipate his every need, while Serena Joy defers to his authority but controls the staff. In their turn the Marthas make Offred's life difficult or easy as they see fit. On a state level control is through advertising techniques and the control of language. An interesting feature of the state's attempts to control every aspect of life is in the head-dress that Offred has to wear. It restricts her vision, giving her a kind of tunnel vision. But in the end it would seem that the real tunnel vision is the weakness of the state of Gilead, unable to see its own mistakes.

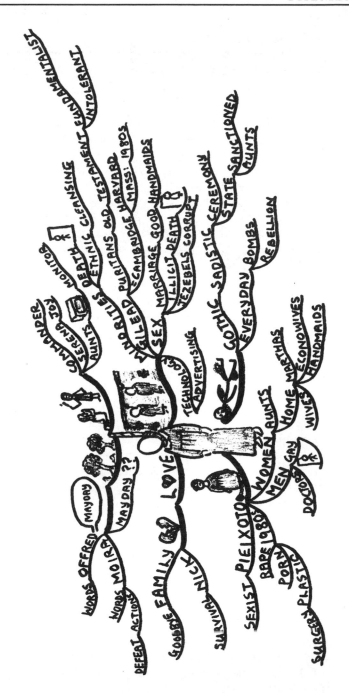

25

L ANGUAGE, STYLE AND STRUCTURE

Imagery

It is when we come to look at the language of the novel that we get an idea of the problems that must have beset Harold Pinter when he came to write the screenplay for the movie. The strength of the novel lies in the inner life of its protagonist, the theme of freedom and resistance being played out inside Offred's mind rather than in dramatic events. The narrative is crowded with imagery, much of it linked together in complex patterns. It is suffused by the colour red: it is the colour of blood and death, as seen on the sack hanging on the Wall, but it is also the colour of fertility, the colour by which Gilead chooses to define its Handmaids, the colour of a fairytale victim and the colour of the tulips in Serena Joy's garden. So the colour merges life, birth and Offred's chances of survival with the continuous possibility of her death if she fails.

The fairytale image of Offred as Little Red Riding Hood merges later with her images of the Commander as a shoemaker in a fairytale, giving Offred's story a fable-like quality and confusing the reader into thinking that just like in a fairytale there will be a resolution. Other sets of images put Offred within a different kind of fable, a sort of Oedipal triangle where the Commander is the paternal figure, offering small treats and forbidden pleasures and Serena Joy is the mother she betrays.

Offred's highly complex sensual life is brought to the fore in her descriptions of Serena Joy's garden in a riot of growth and fertility, smell and heat and texture, linking with the red imagery via the tulips. Also sensual in nature is Offred's concern with food, even the simple food that she is given to eat. Her physical disgust or well-being are reflected in the way she sees her morning breakfast: either sulphurous and faintly disgusting, or whole and attractive. Offred's inner life is one of nature and profusion as opposed to the sterility and technology of Gilead and the men in this society. She sees herself as a swamp or fenland into which she can disappear and where she knows her way around.

Another set of references directs us to the values of the Old Testament. These are rarely called up by Offred; rather they are the way the state justifies its actions and are often used quite ironically by Atwood to highlight its misogyny, so that even the name Gilead has ambiguous associations. The many biblical references link us, via the Word of God and the way that the state twists that to achieve its own ends, to Offred's preoccupation with language and storytelling. Scrabble, the forbidden activity, is of course a word game.

Narrative style

Atwood tells the story in the first person, through the eyes of Offred. Unusually, too, she often uses the present tense, which gives the narrative a feeling of immediacy, as well as a dreamlike quality. Offred's distinctive narrative style dominates the novel, only altering when she recalls the words of the other women whose stories she is telling. Moira's escape story, for example, is told in the way that she thinks Moira would have told it. She adopts other styles too, such as when she describes her encounter with Nick and falls into the clichés of old movies to get herself through an emotional situation with which she is not yet able to deal. Later Offred's gentle, ironic tone is blasted away in the Historical Notes and Professor Pieixoto's academic tone and bad puns about women. ✪ What are the advantages and disadvantages of using Offred as a narrator? How far can we rely on the accuracy of her account, especially given the episodes that she admits to making up.

Structure

Structurally the narrative sits between a set of epigraphs and the Historical Notes, a sort of sandwich. Reading the Historical Notes we realize that Offred's story is a transcription from only partly understood archaic English and may well not be in the correct order since it exists as a series of disjointed tape recordings. The narrative itself seems like the disjointed, fragmented wanderings of a high fever. It shifts about in time alarmingly, with abrupt changes of tense adding to the confusion of readers, often returning repeatedly to the same event, or telling the last half of a story before the first. The reader is forced into an active co-operation with Offred, puzzling out what she is talking about and piecing together the political events behind her personal narrative.

After our intense involvement with Offred and her inner life, the Historical Notes, with their lack of commitment and lack of interest in Offred, come as a shock. Atwood herself has suggested that they add an element of optimism to Offred's story. If Offred survived to make the recordings she must surely have escaped. The irony is of course that even though this is hundreds of years after Offred's death and the demise of Gilead there are still stiff-necked male academics cracking bad jokes about women and dismissing their interests.

Introductory quotations

Genesis 30:1–3

This passage comes from the story of Jacob and his wife Rachel. The barren Rachel tells Jacob to make her servant Bilhah pregnant so that the child will in a sense be Rachel's. This passage represents Gilead's justification for its treatment of certain classes of women. The handmaid in the Bible story, Bilhah, has no say in her planned pregnancy. She is merely a chattel in the patriarchal society depicted here. Rachel, too, has no function beyond childbearing and wishes to be dead rather than childless.

A *quotation from the essay by Jonathan Swift,* A Modest Proposal

This gives a dystopian suggestion to the solutions to the Irish problems of famines and overpopulation – that the babies should be fed to the adults. Atwood proposes a vision of one possible American future in which the problems besetting American society are dealt with but in a way that involves far more inhumanity and suffering than already exists. Like Swift's proposal, this is an exercise in *reductio ad absurdam* – following an idea to its most absurd extreme. She is telling us that Gilead is not so much a dire threat to all our futures as an extension of what already exists.

A *Sufi proverb*

The proverb states the obvious: people don't need to be told not to do what is obviously not good for them. ❂ Why do you think Atwood prefaces her novel with this proverb?

I Night

Chapter 1

◆ An anonymous woman describes a gymnasium where she sleeps.
◆ She recalls being a teenager.

While the women sleep, two Aunts patrol with cattle prods. The anonymous speaker describes a gymnasium, now used as a dormitory but for many generations a place where teenagers played out games of basketball and sexual politics. Offred, as we will come to know her, misses her own past but has no illusions about it. If it meant sex, dances and boyfriends it also meant loneliness, insatiability and disappointment.

In contrast with the freedom of her youth, Offred now sleeps in a row of camp beds, constantly lit and patrolled by women with cattle prods. A clue as to the nature of this new lifestyle is that the patrolling women are not allowed guns; only male guards can carry them. But the male guards in their turn are controlled. They cannot come into the building, while the women are not allowed out except for exercise and in regimented groups. What was once a school now has a high fence and barbed wire and the female inmates are afraid of the men outside.

Over to you

? As the story progresses, Atwood gives us clues about the nature of this society. Find as many quotations as you can which tell us about where this story takes place, what period in time it is, what the nature of this society might be and why these women are imprisoned.

LANGUAGE, STYLE AND STRUCTURE

This brief passage exemplifies much of the style that Atwood has adopted for this novel. The narrator moves freely between her real past, an imagined past of people she has never known but senses in the gymnasium, and the present. We notice though that all these events are narrated in the past tense. They are all memories, creating a complex time structure of the near past (in the gym), the more distant past (her teenage years) and this imaginary past of a society which has gone forever. Here and in the rest of the novel she contrasts the present state with the one that is lost, comparing the two dispassionately, remembering the bad things about the past as well as the good.

Her tone is unemotional; she accepts this new life without complaint, only wishing to make things a little easier. So far she gives little indication of why she is a prisoner. She uses the first person singular only twice to relate her particular memories. For the rest of the narrative she talks about 'we', identifying first with all the other young girls of her generation and then with the other women who are prisoners in the gymnasium.

An aspect of the style of this novel, evident here, is the deliberate way in which Atwood presents us with clues which we must interpret. The feminists of the 1980s talked of the difference between history and 'herstory', men's and women's viewpoints on and interpretations of the events of history. To men, they said, history was about numbers, dates rulers and power systems. Women's history was about minutiae, daily lives and feelings. Here Atwood is clearly placing Offred's tale in the herstory category, at the same time establishing her priorities and making us, the readers, take part in this narrative as we continually try to fathom what has happened both to the USA and to Offred.

II Shopping

Chapter 2

◆ Offred describes her room.
◆ She describes her clothes.
◆ She describes the house.
◆ She prepares to go shopping.

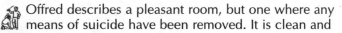 Offred describes a pleasant room, but one where any means of suicide have been removed. It is clean and

bright with a picture on the wall, a window seat, cushions, a polished wooden floor and a folk art rug. She, like the rug which is made from discarded cloth, is being made full use of by 'them', the people who now control her life. She remembers the old expression 'ladies in reduced circumstances', which once meant elderly widows or unmarried daughters who had little income and lived simple, reduced lives. She thinks that she too is one of these. Her circumstances, however, are very different from these genteel Victorian ladies. She wonders if all the others like her have the same features in their rooms and remembers Aunt Lydia telling her to think of it as an army posting.

Weaving through her description is a sense of loss. She thinks of the single bed she sleeps in and talks of rationing her thoughts because too much thinking will prevent her survival. Offred has some freedom in her room. She can take pleasure in the sunlight and the flowers, and comfort herself with the knowledge that although she has little chance of escape she can always choose suicide.

Offred wears a uniform which is completely red, and wings on her head to prevent her looking from side to side, like a horse's blinkers. This introduces one of the extended metaphors of the novel, the colour red, of blood, which, she says, now defines her. The metaphor continues as she sees herself in the pier glass looking like Little Red Riding Hood – and in similar peril.

Here we have the first mention of those who control her life, the Commander and his wife. They too wear uniforms, his black and hers blue, the colour of the Virgin Mary. In the kitchen there are other designations – the Marthas, Rita and Cora. Both wear green and are allowed to use their own names. They are domestic servants in the house. A strict hierarchy exists in this home with the Marthas aloof from Offred.

Again threading through her descriptions is her sense of loss in the 'motherly' sitting room where she is only allowed to kneel, in the sense of possible companionship that she might have with the Marthas. She tells us that while she once would have despised their gossip, now she misses it. In this chapter Luke is mentioned, quite dispassionately, when

Offred remembers a conversation with him about the word 'fraternize'. ✪ This is a memory to Offred. Why does Atwood choose to give her this particular memory?

The gossip of the Marthas fills us in a little about the nature of this society. We have already learned that Offred is a highly controlled person, that she is in danger and that she has suffered a terrible loss. She lives a comfortable life in a wealthy home, which has a Commander, a Wife and two Marthas. ✪ What information do the gossiping Marthas add to this picture? What crimes do they mention?

Chapter 3

◆ Offred sets out through the garden.
◆ She considers the Commander's wife.

Offred gives the first of many descriptions of the garden. It is the end of spring; there are catkins and fading daffodils and the first flush of bright-red tulips, looking like cuts healing. This garden reminds her of the one she once had and she remembers the vitality and freedom she felt handling bulbs and seeds and the smell of ripeness from the soil.

The Commander's Wife seems also to be a figure of reduced circumstances. She is confined by her arthritis, by her own constricting clothing, by her limited horizons. She controls and regiments her garden, orders a Guardian about, and knits complicated scarves for the men who are fighting for the state – the Angels.

The tense changes as Offred remembers her first day at her new posting. It is her third – she has failed in the previous two. The way which the Commander's Wife treats Offred when she first arrives establishes her power over the Handmaid. The details of her power are in the nuances – blocking the doorway, making her carry in her bag, controlling whether she sits or stands.

Suddenly the Wife says something which makes Offred realize who she is, or was: *'It's one of the things we fought for.'* ✪ What does she mean by this? What does it tell you about this woman's role in what has happened? Why does Offred think now that *it was worse than I thought*?

At her first meeting with Serena Joy, Offred feels a sense of loss. She had been hoping that somehow the two women might have felt some bond, perhaps over the desire for a child, or some sisterly solidarity. She realizes that this will not happen. Even in the old days the two women would not have had anything in common.

Chapter 4

◆ Offred encounters Nick.
◆ She meets another Handmaid and they walk to the shops.
◆ They pass through a checkpoint.

There is a brief description of another part of the garden, faintly repellent this time with dying worms *flexible and pink, like lips*, and a lawn divided by a path *like a hair parting*. The cars in this society are named after vaguely religious ideas – Whirlwind, Behemoth, Chariot. The Commander's car is an expensive one, and he has a chauffeur, Nick, who is cleaning it.

Like Serena Joy, Nick trades on the black market, although he is low-status and hasn't been issued a woman. He winks at her and Offred wonders if he is an Eye. ❖ What do you think an Eye is? What does the phrase *he hasn't been issued a woman* tell you about the patriarchal nature of this society?

Offred has not yet told us what her function is in this society, but it seems to involve a great deal of waiting. Here she ponders her life while waiting for her shopping companion. She remembers Aunt Lydia quoting *They also serve who only stand and wait*. Her shopping companion is also dressed in red, and here Offred uses the word Handmaid for the first time. We remember the gymnasium and the 'we' that Offred talked about. Again, there is no comfort or companionship for Offred even with this other Handmaid because their function is to spy on each other. They exchange the official greetings for Handmaids and either Ofglen is afraid of Offred or she is a true believer in her function as a Handmaid.

The women pass through a checkpoint, which gives us an insight into another aspect of this dystopia. Offred reports an earlier overheard conversation between Rita and Cora about a Martha who was shot at this checkpoint because a Guardian thought she had a bomb. The Marthas are aware of the very real threat of someone putting a bomb in the Commander's house and now we see the lengths to which this society has to go to protect its leaders. ✪ Who threatens this state? Is it a real or imagined threat?

At the checkpoint stand two Guardians of the Faith, very young and with a low status in this patriarchal state. Offred is both moved to compassion and afraid of these very young men who have a long time to wait before they will be allocated a woman. When she briefly makes eye contact with one of them, we begin to see that within this regimented society there are small defiant actions such as this which maintain Offred's sense of freedom and hope. Later she moves her hips suggestively as she walks away; another small way of asserting her control over her own body and her resistance to the authority that controls her life.

Offred describes the people and the vehicles that pass through the checkpoint – Commanders, Wives, daughters, Marthas, Handmaids and vans with eyes painted on the side, the secret police perhaps. ✪ Are there any levels of this society that don't pass through this checkpoint? Who are they?

Chapter 5

◆ The women get their groceries.
◆ They see Ofwarren.
◆ They encounter Japanese tourists.

The checkpoint brings the women out of the Commanders' compound into an area that Offred remembers from her past was where doctors and lawyers once lived. She describes regimented front gardens, as if the place were a museum and, notably, an absence of children. We hear more about the war that she has been hinting at and learn the name of the state she lives in – the republic of Gilead. ✪ What indication has there been so far that this is the USA? Which professions are no longer needed in Gilead? Why?

Her thoughts go back to when she and Luke walked around here imagining owning such a house and she is shocked at the freedom that she once had to go where she chose and make choices about her life. The next paragraph introduces us to the class that has so far been missing from this picture of Gilead – the Econowives – married to poor men. ✪ What jobs do you think these poor men might do?

Walking around the busy streets makes Offred think more about her past. She remembers that there were limits to her freedom in the past life. ✪ What were they? Another time-frame intrudes here – her time at the Red Centre, and Aunt Lydia distinguishing between 'freedom from' and 'freedom to'. Now Offred and the other Handmaids have freedom *from*. From *what*? ✪ Do you agree that 1980s America was a society dying of choice?

Even shopping has been altered by the Republic of Gilead. In the past shopping represented choice and a form of power – whether to buy trainers or front-buttoning blouses, jeans or jogging pants. Now shopping has been reduced to collecting whatever food is available. There are no more clothes shops or cosmetics shops. Clothes and shoes are regulation issue. In the early days of Gilead the state gave shops names with biblical overtones – Lilies of the Field, Milk and Honey, All Flesh – but more recently shops have painted out their names, and now just have pictures showing what they sell, in keeping with the state's prohibition on reading.

A little more detail about Gilead emerges. It once controlled central America but still controls California and Florida. Roadblocks and tracks being blown up tells us that there is a sizeable resistance movement even within Gilead's boundaries. ✪ Who do you think the Libertheos might be?

In the shop the food is doled out by Guardians – women don't work in shops any more. The Guardians keep order in the shop also, telling the whispering Handmaids to be silent when they start to talk. In these few minutes of shopping we see how the whole nature of society has been overturned. Where once shops were a place to gossip and make choices, now they are places for menials (all women) to be told what to do by uniformed and armed men.

Ofwarren, or Janine as Offred knows her, is pregnant and another very large piece of the jigsaw falls into place. All the Handmaids are jealous of Ofwarren's condition and

Ofwarren herself enjoys their jealousy. Look at how Offred describes Ofwarren. ◙ Does she feel the same jealousy?

The chicken wrapped in paper sets off another movement in time back to Offred's former life. We realize now that Offred was living with Luke and that they had a child. She shifts into remembering the quarrel they had and then suddenly checks herself – *not here, not now* as if even the memory of a row is too precious to waste here.

The Japanese tourists are titillated at the sight of the Handmaids, about whom they must have heard. Offred, too, is fascinated by the sight of the women with exposed flesh and tortuous shoes. Her response is ambiguous. She doesn't feel the same envy as she did over Ofwarren. Look at how she describes them. ◙ How does she feel?

Chapter 6

◆ Offred and Ofglen walk past the church.
◆ They go to the Wall.
◆ Three doctors who have carried out abortions are hanging from the Wall.

The more we piece together the structure of Gilead, the more it becomes clear that Offred lives the life of a slave. Even her vision has been reduced to fragments both by the wings she wears but also by the unseen but threatening power of the state. We realize that Offred is living in a suburb of a larger city with a subway system linking the suburb with the city, in an area which once had a university campus, a football ground and dormitories for students.

The church makes a link with an even earlier time in history. The church itself no longer functions, but the gravestones have not been altered: as Offred remarks it is only recent history that Gilead wishes to erase. The names on the gravestones are those of Offred's ancestors, and we are put in mind here of the dedication of the novel to Mary Webster, Atwood's own ancestor who was hanged as a witch in the early Puritan colony of Massachusetts. This was a society which had many elements in common with Gilead. There women were kept in the home and those women who asserted authority were called witches and hanged.

Offred and Ofglen walk to the Wall, which surrounds what was once a university football ground but is now used for the men's Salvagings. Hanging from the wall are three bodies of doctors who once performed abortions. To 'salvage' usually means to recover something and make use of it. ✪ What does it mean in Gilead? A picture is emerging of a society run by the fundamentalist Christian right wing where women have been reduced to a biblical role as producers of children and where no woman in her right mind would consider preventing a pregnancy or birth. But far from feeling disgust for these men, Offred feels an affinity with them. They are, she says, time travellers from the past.

Offred's chief feeling is one of relief that none of these men is Luke. She considers the connections. She becomes disoriented, feeling that there is a connection between the bloody mouth on the sack covering one of the victims' heads and the tulips in Serena Joy's garden, but steadies herself. She knows that in order to stay sane she must accept each thing she sees for what it is. She remembers another of Aunt Lydia's sayings: *this may not seem ordinary to you now, but after a time it will. It will become ordinary.*

Over to you

? At the end of this novel is a discussion which takes place centuries after the fall of Gilead. Offred's narrative provides source material for the historical reconstruction of Gilead. Under the following headings write an objective account of Gilead using information you have gleaned from this section of the novel:

Social strata
Values
Crime and punishment
Economy and currency
Role of the Handmaids
Importance of dress
Known political events
Relations with other states

Leave some space in this account to add material as you learn it. You might want to colour code later information or indicate exactly where the information appears.

? Like the society of George Orwell's novel *1984*, Gilead has changed parts of the language to suit its needs. Give Gilead definitions for the following words and expressions:

      Econowives
      Salvagings
      Angels
      Eye
      Blessed be the fruit
      May the Lord open
      Compucheck
      Prayvaganzas
      Birthmobiles

? Offred's life has been reduced to the barest of activities. Draw a Mind Map for Offred with each branch showing an aspect of her life – the past, shopping, the Commander's house, the Red Centre, etc. Leave space to add to the Mind Map. Which branch do you think will be extended the most? As you add material you might want to indicate where in the novel the information appears.

? Critics point out that this is not just one woman's story: Offred also tells the stories of other women's repression. Serena Joy is one of these. Make a Mind Map for Serena Joy showing what we know about her so far – appearance, current activities, past life, character. As you learn more about her, add further details. You might want, later, to use colour-coding to show where in the novel the new information emerged.

LANGUAGE, STYLE AND STRUCTURE

As we have seen, the state of Gilead has created some new words and altered the meanings of others. *Salvage* now means execute, an *Aunt* is a cattle-prod-wielding prison officer, while *Angels* are the military arm of the state. The official Handmaid greetings are biblical quotations and there are sanctioned topics, such as the success of the war, as well as sanctioned responses, such as *praise be, which I receive with joy.* Shops are named after passages from the Bible too, but again are distorted. Lilies, a shop selling Gilead-approved women's clothes, comes from a passage in Mark: *Consider the Lilies of the field; they toil not, neither do they spin.* In this passage, Mark exhorts people not to be concerned with the necessities of life because God will provide for them. All Flesh, the butcher's shop, comes from a passage in Isiah in which the phrase refers to all humanity. Here it means meat.

Biblical passages are used to justify the state's treatment of women, even if it means distorting the meaning of the texts, or even, as occurs later in the novel, misquoting them. Offred points out that there is a biblical precedent for hitting Handmaids, although she doesn't tell us what it is. Mixed in with the biblical echoes are modernisms of the 1980s: *birthmobile* reminds us of the popemobile or batmobile, both futuristic expressions, while *Prayvaganzas* suggests the language of advertising, which often makes up new words by combining existing ones: here 'prayer' and 'extravaganza' are combined. *Econowives* is a similar construction.

The newly fledged state is learning how best to control its citizens and seems to be moving into a new stage of understanding about control. Where at first it referred to the Bible to justify its actions, now Offred notes that all written language is being erased. The shops no longer carry their names, and the tokens carry only pictures, in preparation for the time when Handmaids, perhaps all women, can no longer read.

Sitting alongside this official Gilead speak is the language of subversion and dissent – seen in the Marthas' gossip about toilet cleaner, knitting needles and the death of one of their fellow servants, the silent lip-reading of the women in the Red Centre, as well as Offred's cynical and bitter commentary on her experiences. Offred's concern with language centres around her desperate need to regain some feeling of control over her own life and her silent subverting of the state's values: *these are the kinds of litanies I use, to compose myself* she says much later in the novel. In her passive state in her room she thinks about the language people used to use – *I hear where you're coming from* is an expression she remembers, thinking that it suggests travel, an activity forbidden to Offred. *Ladies in reduced circumstances* is another phrase from the past that she recalls and she remembers Luke saying there was no female equivalent of the word 'fraternize'. She remembers old expressions such as *I smell a rat,* or *fishy.* It is as if remembering details of the old ways are her form of resistance: if she can keep her old life in her head she has some control over her present condition – a form of resistance to the state.

The imagery in which Atwood chooses to communicate Offred's feelings is beginning to emerge. The colour red symbolizes life and fruitfulness as well as danger. The tulips are both burgeoning flowers and healing cuts, while Offred herself is Little Red Riding Hood, a child in terrible danger, and a *sister dipped in blood,* one of a religious sisterhood. The contradictory nature of the image repeats in the bloody smile on the cloth covering one of the hanged doctors. Offred wears red shoes like Dorothy in the *Wizard of Oz,* but they are not magical. In modern culture red is an aggressive colour often associated with passion and flirtatiousness (think of Curly's wife in Steinbeck's *Of Mice and Men*), and strangely this society has chosen to clothe its most secret possessions in this gaudy colour. Offred remembers Aunt Lydia reminding the Handmaids that to be seen is to be penetrated.

When Offred describes her surroundings or the events of her day her tone is largely dispassionate. She carefully excludes all emotion which might give her away, but her soul emerges in the way she describes certain things. For example, her ambiguous response to the Japanese women emerges as she describes them, first of all as if they were robins, tiny, chirpy, engaged in life. She sees the displayed sexuality of these women in a complex combination of admiration and disgust – their legs are *nearly* naked. There is a kind of prurience here, seeing sex where it isn't intended. Their feet are in spiked heels throwing them off balance as if they were on stilts and their buttocks are thrust outward. There is nothing attractive here – it sounds more like an anthropologist's description of animals' mating rituals.

The next sentence, describing the Japanese women's hair, feels more as if Offred is reminded of the pleasure of sexuality, while the red lipstick they wear is again an ugly image of graffiti, with the suggestion of an obscenity on a toilet wall. Later she describes the woman's feet and her description is full of a sense of loss and sensuousness. Atwood has here shown us rather than told us that Offred is partly indoctrinated by Gilead. Her response is part disgust that a woman should display herself in that way, and part longing for the past.

Atwood's style forces the reader into a very unfamiliar kind of reading activity. She pitches us straight into the story without explanations. At first we don't even know what Offred's exact function is, although we can make an educated guess from the opening epigrams. We have to guess at Offred's past life and much of her present circumstances. Like the academics at the end of the novel we are forced to engage with Offred, to interpret what is going on, to pick up on tiny clues. Atwood's reasons for doing this will be discussed later, but it is enough to realize that we are not passive readers of a good story here – we are engaged in the plot. ✪ Many critics have suggested that Offred's real name has already been told us. Do you know what it is?

Test yourself

❓ Look at Offred's descriptions of (a) Serena Joy's garden and (b) the pregnant Ofwarren, and make a Mind Map of the descriptions showing the way the imagery used portrays the complexity of Offred's feelings.
❓ Write a brief version of the political and personal events which have happened in Offred's life as we know them so far.

Take a break. Go down the High St and indulge in a little shopping therapy.

III Night

Chapter 7

◆ Offred remembers Moira at college.
◆ She remembers a childhood incident with her mother.
◆ She remembers a time after she had lost her daughter.

The night is Offred's own time, which she uses to re-establish her freedom by recalling her past. She chooses a happy time for her when she was a student. She remembers the words she and her friends spoke, but examines the room she was in with curiosity at the freedoms that she once took for granted – an unmade bed, cigarettes, books all over the floor, an essay on date rape.

Her second memory is from an earlier time in the park with her mother. This memory has mixed emotions associated with it – anger that her mother had tricked her and lied to her, but pleasure at the thought of the fire and the delight she saw on people's faces. ✪ Do these two memories have anything in common?

Her next memory is involuntary. Something about her exploration of her pleasant memories has triggered this next one. This memory is less clear, and unlike the others where she is storytelling, giving names and describing events, this is a series of broken images as if it is more direct, not mediated through Offred's storytelling activities. There are no names, just *they* and *I* and *her*. The location isn't clear – it might be a hospital or prison, and the responses of the people around her are ambiguous – they show her a photograph of 'her' and sympathetically say that she has had a shock but equally gently they tell the woman who was to become Offred that she is unfit to be a mother.

These three memories are framed within Offred's thoughts about what she is doing. Her initial thoughts are about her passivity – she thinks about the words *lie* and *lay*, the one active and the other passive and she acknowledges that her only freedoms occur when she is at her most passive, laying still in the allotted time and place.

Her final thoughts are about what she is doing retelling her memories like this. She considers that it might be storytelling, but accepts that if it were she could control the ending so admits that this is not storytelling – there is no one there to read her story. If it were a letter Offred was writing in her head it might put the recipient in great danger. ✪ Does she have someone in mind when she says she will write to *Dear you*?

IV Waiting room

*C*hapter 8

◆ Offred sees a funeral.
◆ Nick speaks to her.
◆ The Commander is standing looking into her room.

Offred takes up her story the next day at the place where she left off – the Wall. There are more bodies: a priest and two Angels hanged for homosexuality. Another snippet of history emerges – there have been sect wars at some time in the recent past. A funeral procession goes by for a miscarried foetus of perhaps three months. What seems normal – a funeral – has been distorted by this dystopian society to include what our society would barely consider a death at all. ✪ Consider Aunt Lydia's proposition that one day when times improve no one will have to be an Econowife – is this feasible? Who would do the housework? In the previous chapter Offred notes that there used to be women dressed in black. What do you think has happened to them?

Nick greets Offred, breaking the rules by doing so and putting both of them in danger. Offred has already spotted something fishy about Nick – he is too confident, he doesn't behave in a servile way so perhaps he is an Eye and this greeting is to test her. Offred trusts no one. Nick's greeting disturbs another memory of Offred's – Aunt Lydia's quotation, *All flesh is weak*. She is misquoting the Bible and Offred corrects her, *All flesh is grass*. The misquote is not an idle one for Atwood. *All flesh is grass* is from Isiah 40:6, which suggests that in the sight of the majesty of God all humans are like the grass – they will wither, whereas God is eternal. Offred silently reminds Lydia that even she and her controllers are mortal, just like Offred. Lydia's misquote suggests that *all flesh* refers only to men who are not mortal but weak. Women have been excluded.

We get another instalment in the life story of Serena Joy, originally Pam. Dedicated to religious right-wing beliefs, she spent her time promulgating the theory that a woman's place is in the home, an idea that tends to become fashionable when jobs are in short supply. The assassination attempt suggests how powerful the theories of the right wing had become. Offred amuses herself with the irony of Serena Joy's situation – now she finds herself practising what she preaches and doesn't seem too pleased about it. Like the Handmaids, the Econowives, and the Marthas, the Wives also live restricted lives. ❂ If all the women live in reduced circumstances, and the Guardians like Nick have to hope to be allotted a wife, and the Angels are fighting an unpleasant war, who does benefit from this society?

In Section II of the novel, the previous day, Offred goes through the kitchen as Rita is making bread. Offred's story stops at the Wall and begins there again the next day. When she returns, Rita has finished making the next day's bread. We can see from this the monotony of Offred's life in which one day melds into the next with very little distinction.

Chapter 9

◆ Offred remembers the early days of her relationship with Luke.
◆ She describes how she examined the room.
◆ She finds the message.
◆ She asks Rita about the previous Handmaid.

Offred has finished her day's work – the shopping – and now goes to the room where she waits. She has accidentally called it 'her' room and now considers it more carefully. First, though, the way she examines this room reminds her of the old days when she was careless about her freedom and could make phone calls, write postcards or order room service. She looks back on those days which seemed to her at the time to be full of worry, and she now knows that in fact she was free and happy, but took all she had for granted. She remembers *an attack of the past*, which is different from her careful selection of times to remember in the previous section of the novel. Here she is overcome with a sense of loss, and we understand why she wants Rita's knife and thinks about shatterproof glass.

The message she discovers from the last Handmaid is an act of resistance to the state of Gilead, although Offred doesn't know what it means. The thought of this act of resistance reminds her of Moira. When she asks Rita about the previous Handmaid, Rita refuses to talk about her.

Chapter 10

◆ Still in her room Offred remembers singing and sunbathing.
◆ A story comes to her from her past about Moira.
◆ She recalls the newspaper stories about sexual assaults and murders.
◆ Looking down at the Commander getting into his car she remembers another story about Moira.

Atwood is taking us through what life is like for Offred, who spends most of her time in her room with nothing to do. Her enforced stillness allows her to move back in time to her other life. First she remembers Moira suggesting they have a sexy underwear party which stands in sharp contrast to Offred's memory of her mother burning pornographic magazines. We realize that in this novel Atwood is not only examining a possible dystopic future of control and suppression, but also the quite real threads of feminism which she imagines will have led up to this dystopia. Moira is a different kind of feminist to Offred's mother. ❂ Can you see at this stage of the novel what the differences are between Moira and Offred's mother? Make a Mini Mind Map.

Offred is forbidden to read but her new owners have left a cushion in her room embroidered with the word *faith*. Its two accompanying words, possibly once embroidered on other cushions, *hope* and *charity*, have gone. ❂ What is the irony in this word surviving while the others have disappeared?

Offred remembers another event with Moira – throwing water bombs out of her dorm window. The memory marks an early stage in the right-wing backlash against equality for men and women – the dorms were single sex where once they had been co-ed.

Chapter 11

32001

◆ Offred visits the gynaecology clinic.
◆ The gynaecologist offers to make her pregnant.

Here we see more of the foolish new rules that Gilead has established. The gynaecologist must not see his patient. We are reminded of practices in strongly religious societies in the Far East and Middle East where women are kept from the gaze of all men, even their doctors. The nurse is a man wearing a gun – the only women who work outside the home in this society are the Aunts.

We discover that Offred has only a limited time in which to conceive a child – the gynaecologist offers to impregnate her knowing that she is desperate for a child. He utters the word *sterile* which shocks her. In this society it is illegal to suggest that men may be unable to father a child. Only women are to be blamed for the absence of children.

Offred is put into a distressing situation by the doctor's offer. If she takes it up and is found out she could be executed. If she refuses she may never conceive and will have to face the consequences. If she offends the doctor he can falsify her report to say she cannot conceive and have her sent to the Colonies with the Unwomen. ✪ This is the first time that the Colonies and the Unwomen have been mentioned. What do you think they are?

Offred quotes part of the opening quotation of the novel *Give me children or else I die*, the words of Rachel regretting her barrenness in Genesis 30:1. ✪ In Offred's case the quotation takes on a different meaning. What is it?

Chapter 12

◆ Offred takes a bath.
◆ She eats dinner.

We are aware now that all the waiting, the visit to the doctor and now the bath are a preparation for something. Atwood is building up to some as yet undisclosed event.

We do not know what it will be but our imaginations are surely filled with horror at what might be about to happen to her – some sexual depravity or humiliation. All references to violence so far have been state violence – cold and deliberate acts perpetrated against people we would consider innocent, and done in the name of God. We can't yet foresee this event but in the context of Gilead it surely will be something cold and violent.

As with a Victorian Gothic novel where we see the heroine heading towards some horror but can do nothing to stop it, we watch while Offred goes through a ritual bathing in preparation for an act which is to be carried out on her body. As she gets in the bath she refuses to look at her body which is no longer hers – it is tattooed and has become a national resource. Later, as she is dressing, another memory of watching women have their heads shaved as a punishment adds to our sense of impending violence. ✪ What is it about Offred that makes her a national resource? What do the tattooed ankle and the memory of women having their heads shaved have in common?

Here is the most poignant memory so far. In the bath she remembers the smell of her daughter. The memory is described in the present tense – to Offred the memory is so strong that it seems as if the child is actually present. She also remembers another event in the progress towards this state run by the religious right. A woman steals her baby from a supermarket trolley claiming that God had told her to do it. At the time it had seemed like a freak event but remembered from the perspective of Offred's present existence it is more significant.

Offred loses her memory of her daughter and plays with the idea of how it would have been if the child had died rather than been taken away by a fascist state. She imagines going through old photographs and mementoes of the child and briefly wonders what has happened to all her things. She remembers one of Aunt Lydia's sayings, *blessed are the meek*, ironically recalling the rest of the quotation, left out by Lydia, *for they shall inherit the earth* (Matthew 5:5). We see the double standards of this hypocritical society which teaches the Handmaids poverty of spirit while encouraging the

Commanders to live lives of luxury with servants and beautiful possessions.

Later Cora brings her food and it reminds us of a condemned person eating a last meal. Offred is very tense – she cannot eat the food but has to force it down. She has so little control over her own life that she can be punished for not eating. Offred recalls another of Lydia's misquotations *May the Lord make us truly grateful* – the old expression was *thankful*. ❸ What is the difference between those two words?

Over to you

? Aunt Lydia and her teaching at the Red Centre recur frequently in Offred's memory. Go back over the novel so far and find references to her. Make a Mind Map of information about her – her appearance, her behaviour, her sayings. What do you think she might have been in the time before Gilead? Why would she take part in a system which has created female slavery?

? Offred is surrounded by people whom she cannot trust, because they believe entirely in the Gilead system, because they are afraid to oppose it, or because they are completely cynical and are exploiting it. For each of the characters in the list below choose one of the categories describing their attitudes to Gilead and its values.

committed   accepting   disillusioned   exploiting
afraid   undermining

Offred	Aunt Lydia
Serena Joy	Nick
Commander	Rita
Ofwarren	Cora
Ofglen	Moira

You may want to return to these divisions later in the novel and reappraise your decisions.

? How believable do you find Gilead? Is it possible for such a transformation of society to have occurred in a period of about four to five years? We know that a woman tried to steal Offred's baby, that college dorms were made single sex even in Offred's youth, and that there had been a movement aimed at getting women confined to the home as they had been in Victorian times. If we add the cataclysmic fall in birthrate in the USA that is being hinted at here is it possible for this to have happened? Look at the following list of things which Offred has mentioned and say what has happened to them in Gilead. For each one say whether you think these things are credible: cinema, fashion, beauty products, universities, childbirth, football, reading, cigarettes, alcohol, cars.

? The manufacturers of clothes, cosmetics, recreational drugs, movies and cars are powerful, wealthy institutions in the USA. What would they have to say about a society in which none of these things are freely available to the masses any more? Would a state, even one like Gilead, murder a valuable resource such as the doctors we saw hanging on the Wall or send barren women to the Colonies when they could be made better use of at home? Does it matter that Gilead should be believable?

? Make a list of the new pieces of information about Offred's past life which you have learned in this section.

LANGUAGE, STYLE AND STRUCTURE

Atwood tells us the story of Offred and her life, in modern USA and Gilead, in a series of broken blocks, interspersed with sections called 'Night' where Offred has time to reflect on what has happened to her. The 'Night' sections are her own time when she can move back into her past and relive it. She recalls things in a seemingly disjointed way, but there is a careful structure to the snippets of past life and the many unexplained references. We read this novel like a detective story, working out what has happened to Offred, what might happen to her, how the strange state of Gilead could have come about. As we have said before, this is intentional on Atwood's part. We become like the anthropologists at the end of the novel, assessing the state and Offred's role in it, through, and almost in spite of, Offred's concerns about her past and her feelings.

In this section several images return. As Offred returns to the house from her shopping trip she watches Serena Joy in the garden. The tulips are still there but now they are in full bloom, *redder than ever*. They have become like Offred, an open chalice offering itself up but empty, and will be destroyed themselves once their function is fulfilled. Serena Joy is watching them and we get the sense of threat to Offred in that watching. It is the Wife that Offred has to fear, not the Commander. Some critics have pointed out that Serena Joy is like an evil mother figure – perhaps a wicked stepmother, gnarled and arthritic with anger and frustration and full of malevolence towards the daughter figure, Offred.

Offred herself notices the tulips but makes no connection between herself and them. It is her way, critics have suggested, of denying what is happening to her. Earlier, at the Wall, she has denied that there are any connections between the tulips and the bloody mouth on the hanging figure. If Offred admits that she is like the tulips, empty, open to penetration, disposable, or like the bloody mouth, dead, she will be unable to live in this reality. At the Wall she says: *It is through a field of such valid objects that I must make my way, every day, in every way. I put a lot of effort into such distinctions. I need to make them.*

At the end of Chapter 8, when Offred goes to her room the Commander is standing at the door and Offred sees him for a few moments as a wild animal, perhaps a wolf – *lowered eyelids, ears laid back, raised hackles. A flash of bared teeth ...*

V Nap

Chapter 13

◆ Offred waits to be summoned downstairs.
◆ She remembers Moira arriving at the Red Centre.
◆ She dreams about Luke.
◆ She remembers losing her daughter.

Offred has nothing to do until she is summoned downstairs and she reflects on the nature of boredom. In nineteenth-century oil paintings, harems of exotic women were displayed in a similar state to her own – waiting to be called into sexual service. In the paintings the sense of waiting was erotic but to Offred it is a sign of the lack of control she has over her life. She feels she is like a laboratory or farmed animal. ✪ Look at the image she uses to describe her state of mind: *thin white dancers … their legs fluttering like the wings of held birds.* How does this image help to show us how she feels?

After only three weeks at the Red Centre, Offred has learned how to resist the system in a small way. She has places where she can find a few moments privacy and has learned when the Aunts are inattentive.

We see the way that the Aunts have taken over the minds of the women at the centre. Even Offred joins in the persecution of Janine (whom she knows in Gilead as Ofwarren). To keep silent is dangerous to herself but that isn't why she joins in. Offred stops her story about Moira just as she is about to talk to her. ✪ Why?

Offred slips into sleep and dreams about her old apartment and Luke. Her clothes no longer fit and she cannot communicate with her husband. This dream segues into a sharper, more real memory of running through woods with her daughter, pursued by people with guns.

Now try this

? How much of Offred's life can you reconstruct from what you have learned so far? Is it possible to estimate what year/decade she was born? What do we know about her education, marriage, work, her daughter? What year might the events in Gilead be taking place? How old is she now? Where, in the real USA, is the school that becomes the Red Centre? Why was she running away with her daughter? Draw up a Curriculum Vitae for Offred. Leave spaces for information you don't have. You can fill it in as more information emerges.

LANGUAGE, STYLE AND STRUCTURE

The Gilead plot is suspended for a time as Offred sits in her room. This gives Atwood an opportunity for some reflective writing and some catching up with the earlier narrative lines – Offred in the USA that we know and her time at the Red Centre. We are still given the bare outline of events. How Gilead came about is still quite mysterious. Atwood here focuses on imagery which was begun earlier – Offred as a body. Offred contrasts her current blank time with the things she used to do when she was free. Now she says that her body is no longer the same to her; it is a dangerous place, a swamp where only Offred knows the safe routes. Like a Native American putting her ear to the ground, she listens to her body to find out what her future will be.

Now try this

? Make a Mind Map of the passage beginning *I sink down into my own body* showing the various threads of the metaphor which Offred uses to describe her body. Notice the similarities here in the imagery of red flowers between Atwood and the poet Sylvia Plath.

Have a rest. Lie, down, put Chopin's Les Sylphides on the CD player, and listen to the sounds of your body.

VI Household

Chapter 14

- ◆ Offred goes downstairs to the sitting room.
- ◆ She watches the news on television.
- ◆ She remembers her bid to escape.

Offred describes in detail a rich but sterile room full of luxury items but where nothing ever happens. Serena Joy has lost almost as much as Offred has since the Gilead regime took over. Although it is called a sitting room, even the posture of its occupants is controlled. Offred must kneel while the other servants stand behind her, ready for the much awaited Ceremony. Sometimes, Offred tells us, Serena Joy leans on her shoulder as she sits down – Offred has become a possession, like the furniture, rather than an individual with rights.

The television news fills in some background about Gilead for us. Like George Orwell's *1984* there is a continual war but not as in Orwell's novel between three superpowers but in scattered parts of the USA. The enemies are Baptists and Quakers. The Children of Ham (black people?) are being resettled in a distant rural area – North Dakota – where there is nothing for them, rather in the same way as the Nazis suggested the Jews be resettled in Madagascar. The Quakers are accused of smuggling precious national resources over the border to Canada. This must make Offred feel better – she is one of those national resources.

Suddenly in mid-sentence Offred is involuntarily reliving the time when she lost her daughter. She, Luke and the child are driving to the border with Canada with fake passports. We already know the end result of this trip – the gunshots and struggle she remembered in the last section. There are already control posts looking for escaping people. Why does Atwood have Offred tell us this story here, while she waits for the Ceremony?

Chapter 15

- ◆ The Commander reads from the Bible.
- ◆ Offred remembers Moira's first attempt to escape from the Red Centre.

The household are lined up in the sitting room waiting for the Commander to arrive; Offred is on her knees. We wonder if this is the Ceremony, or some group ritual, but that sounds a little kinky for this fundamentalist state. Instead, following protocol which has been established perhaps over several years, the Commander takes a Bible out of a locked box and reads some relevant sections about producing offspring.

While the Commander reads, Offred wanders off into her own mental world again. She considers what it must mean to be a man in this society – 'sized up' by watching women, all of whom react to his every move and are completely dependent on him. The Commander's Bible readings send Offred back to her time at the Red Centre when the same passage from Genesis was read. Other passages are also read, many of them changed to suit the Handmaids' indoctrination process. As we have seen from the sitting room scene, the Word is now locked up so the Handmaids cannot query it. Moira's plan is to fake illness, get herself sent to hospital and then offer the Guardian Angels in the ambulance sex in exchange for her freedom. Her plan fails and she is brought back and tortured. ○ Why do you think Atwood plays this memory against the background of the Commander reading?

Much of this chapter focuses on the Commander and how Offred feels about him. He is first a semi-retired museum guard, then a bank manager, then a strong-jawed model in a vodka ad. Later she sees him as a fairytale shoemaker. As he reads, Offred imagines it as a bedtime story, so the Commander becomes a father figure with his children.

These are all fairly innocuous, kind images of a man who wields enormous power in a fascist state. Offred tells us that the innocuousness is false. *One false move and I'm dead*, she says. The joke carries many layers of meaning. This man is also vulnerable in this state and if he falls from power she will suffer. We know that if he fails to make her pregnant she will go to the Colonies. Also if she makes a false move, fails to please in some way, he can end her life.

While the reading takes place, Serena Joy begins to cry. They are genuine tears – she tries to hold them back. The effect on the rest of the household is to make them stifle laughter and there is something humiliatingly funny, *like a fart in church*, about this middle-aged woman weeping in front of her servants in advance of some act of procreation. ✪ What is Serena Joy crying for? Do you feel pity for her? Does Offred?

We have already noted the disturbing violence of Moira's treatment at the hands of the Aunts. They hurt her feet and hands because these are not necessary to breeding. Handmaids no longer need them since they no longer do anything or go anywhere. There is also the muted, suggested violence and disgust in Offred's series of phallic images, and in the connection between Moira's torture and the image of the Commander as a boot enclosing a pulpy tender foot.

Chapter 16

◆ Offred describes the Ceremony.

This is the scene that the novel has been building towards for several chapters. ✪ What expectations did you have before you read it? Rape? Humiliation? Instead we are given an almost humorous description, nearly slapstick in the arrangement of bodies and the way in which it has been made as unenjoyable as possible for all concerned. What should have been an erotic male sexual fantasy – two women in bed at the same time – becomes a chore: unpleasant but not cruel, perhaps even rather boring.

Offred's chief feeling seems to be gratitude that this Commander doesn't smell bad like the previous one. Offred spends the time thinking her own thoughts, the Commander is distracted and distant while Serena Joy seems the most emotionally involved in what is happening. After it is over Offred's instinct is to laugh. ✪ If Serena Joy is the symbolic wicked stepmother and the Commander is a kind of father figure, what is actually being played out here?

Chapter 17

◆ Offred rubs butter saved from dinner on her hands and face.
◆ She goes downstairs to the sitting room and steals a daffodil.
◆ Nick tells her the Commander wants to see her.

The state which runs Offred's life has given itself the name Gilead. The name comes from one of the names of the twelve tribes of Israel. It features in the Negro spiritual song *There is a balm in Gilead to heal the sin-sick soul*, making the name represent a good and holy place. But a closer reading of the Bible reveals Gilead to be a fairly wicked place. In the original Bible text, Jeremiah asks *Is there no balm in Gilead; is there no physician there? Why then is not the health of the daughter of my people more recovered?* The Gilead of Jeremiah is a place where the daughter is not protected and looked after. Here, rubbing butter into her skin, Offred is illustrating in very physical terms that there is no balm (or face cream!) in Gilead, a wicked joke on Atwood's part.

After the travesty of the sex, the humour with which Offred usually keeps herself going has worn a little thin but we still see it in *buttered, I lie on my single bed like a piece of toast*. But the act has brought home to her even more than usual how alone and unloved she is. She goes to look at the moon and contrasts what it looks like – a goddess, a wink, a sliver of ancient rock – with what it really is: a stone surrounded by lethal weaponry.

As she goes downstairs Offred imagines herself as a wild animal. The sitting room becomes a wood where she takes a magic flower – the dying cut daffodil. Offred has come downstairs looking for some act of rebellion, some way of showing that she is alive and has her own life. Suddenly it is presented to her in the form of Nick. Compare the passion and sensuality of these few seconds of physical contact with the ugly scene described in the previous chapter. Both know that they could be killed for what they have done but they have risked it anyway. Offred has found the thing that she came downstairs to find.

LANGUAGE, STYLE AND STRUCTURE

Offred, whose name appears in this section of the novel for the first time, has two styles of narrative; one in which she reports objectively the things she sees around her, and another where her feelings strongly affect what she sees and describes. The objective style is Offred's way of staying sane in this insane society (and Atwood's way of describing the minutiae of Gilead) and the imaginative writing allows us to experience Offred's real feelings which she transposes onto her surroundings. In Chapter 14, for example, she describes Serena Joy's sitting room in terms which express her fear of, and contempt and repulsion for, her owners. So as she waits, kneeling, she describes it as a parlour, *the kind with spiders and flies*, reminding us of the nursery rhyme as well as focusing on her vulnerable, victim-like state.

The stultifying nature of the family life in the house is transposed onto the features of the room, enforced by the use of words like *subdued* and *mutely*; the room is like a cave with its furniture *crusting and hardening* into fixed forms. The women in the paintings are *stiff, their breasts constricted, their faces pinched...* and there is much more along the same lines. Offred sees herself as a waif in a fairytale, a victim, and later in Chapter 17 as a wild animal. In Chapter 15 while she waits for the Commander to begin reading, Offred spirals off into a fantasy of phallic images, and we get a strong sense of her disgust for this man's role on her life. ❂ Why do you think these phallic images are here in Chapter 15 rather than in the next chapter where the sexual act actually takes place?

It is also useful to look at the structure of these chapters. In the previous sections very few events have actually taken place in the present. Offred has been in her room recalling her past. Now the thrust of the storyline comes back to the present and we see the whole household grouped together, and the Commander in particular. Set against this apparently kindly man is the story of the violence perpetrated against Moira by the state that he represents. In this section we also have another piece of her own escape attempt with her husband and daughter. That story is left suspended as they drive towards the border in just the same way that Offred is suspended in the sitting room, waiting for some inevitable and ugly act to take place.

It is in this section of the novel also that the narrative line moves predominantly into the present. With the secret meeting of Nick and his orders from the Commander we can see that the humdrum routine of Offred's life is about to change; whether for the better or worse is not yet clear.

Now try this

? Draw a Mind Map for the Commander, using Offred's images as well as your knowledge of his role in this society. You could add each of the other members of the household to this map, showing their relationship with him. The Mind Map has been started for you below.

? Look at the following quotations and say for each of them what they tell us about (a) Offred's state of mind, and (b) the person with whom they are connected:

1 *When the bell has finished I descend the stairs, a brief waif in the eye of the glass that hangs on the downstairs wall. The clock ticks with its pendulum, keeping time; my feet in their neat red shoes count the way down.*

2 *It makes me feel slightly ill, as if I'm in a closed car on a hot muggy day with an older woman wearing*

too much face powder.

3 *I feel the shoe soften, blood flows into it, it grows warm, it becomes a skin.*

4 *No use for you, I think at her, my face unmoving, you can't use them any more, you're withered. They're the genital organs of plants ...*

5 *Now he looks like a shoemaker in an old fairytale book.*

6 *It makes an exhausted sound like a padded door shutting ... like papier poudre, pink and powdery from the time before ... in those stores that sold candles and soap in the shape of things ... and the Commander fucks, with a regular two-four marching stroke, on and on like a tap dripping.*

7 *In the hall the nightlight's on, the long space glows gently pink; I walk one foot set carefully down, then the other, without creaking along the runner as if on a forest floor, sneaking, my heart quick, through the night house.*

In particular compare the two descriptions of Offred going downstairs and say why they are so different.

? Look at the following statements and give them a score of 1–5 according to how far you agree with them (0 = completely disagree). Try to say why you have given each statement its score.

Offred is an unwilling victim of the state of Gilead. Every month when she is at her most fertile she is raped by the Commander.

She is too frightened to resist her oppressors.

Serena Joy would prefer things to be the same as they were when she was on television.

Gilead is ruled by men who believe that the values of the Old Testament are very important.

Only those men and women who run the state of Gilead benefit from it.

It would be better to rebel and be sent to the Colonies than to suffer Offred's fate.

This state would never exist in reality. No one would support it.

The Marthas have a better life now than they did
in the old days.
Everything this state tells people is the truth.

*Before you go on to the next section take a
break – make a coffee, rub some body
lotion on your hands, switch on the TV –
and be thankful you're not Offred!*

VII Night

Chapter 18

◆ Offred thinks about what may have happened to Luke.

💔 The sudden meeting with Nick has shocked Offred. She
found herself overcome with desire for a complete
stranger, and feels as if it is a betrayal of Luke whom she both
desired and loved. The shame of her feelings forces her into
thinking what has happened to Luke. We can tell from her
rehearsed telling of the story that she has covered this ground
many times before. She has three theories about what has
happened to him. The first, the most likely, is that the shots she
heard when she was captured killed him and his body lies still
where he was shot down. Worse still, in many ways, is her
belief that he has been captured and for some reason (she
can't think of one) he is being kept alive and tortured. This
thought at least gives her some hope that there might be a
happy ending to the story she is telling. Her third belief, or
daydream almost, is that Luke escaped and is in Canada
working towards rescuing her and that all three of them will be
together again some day – that there is a resistance movement
and a chance of living beyond her present misery.

What emerges from these dreams is the feelings of guilt that
Offred has that she is physically well and relatively safe while
Luke may be dead or suffering. ✪ Which of her theories about
Luke do you think is the most likely? Why? Can you think of
what else may have happened to him? Offred has often
contemplated suicide. Why doesn't she kill herself?

VIII Birth day

Chapter 19

◆ Offred eats her breakfast.
◆ The red birthmobile arrives for her.
◆ She remembers the lectures on childbirth at the Red Centre.
◆ She imagines the Commanders' Wives talking about their Handmaids.

Offred wakes up badly, dreaming repeatedly that she is in other realities. Her mood is sombre, disillusioned and she considers the small pleasures that she now has – eating an egg, for example. Offred considers the word *chair* and thinks that there are no connections between the object and the other things associated with it – execution in an electric chair, the French word for flesh, the leader of a meeting, the first syllable of charity. ○ Is she right or is she still refusing to make connections?

Suddenly the whole course of the day is altered by the birthmobile siren and we see again the odd mix of dissent and happiness that the prospect of a birth gives her. The other Handmaids are excited, almost hysterical because for today at least many of the restrictions on their lives will be lifted. A change, as they say, is as good as a rest.

As she travels to the birth, Offred rehearses some of the history of Gilead – how the birthrate fell sharply because of pollution, the effects of chemical weapons and some catastrophic earthquakes in the west. Most people are so badly affected by the poisonous atmosphere that they are sterile. Only a few women are now fertile and these become the Handmaids. The impossibly sudden changeover to the society that now exists in the USA becomes much more feasible in the light of this emergency, as do the hangings of abortionists.

When Offred arrives at Ofwarren's, the doctors who once attended births are in a van outside. Technology such as sonar scans, induced labour, anaesthetics, prenatal testing is no longer associated with childbirth. Gilead has ruled that women must suffer in childbirth as they did in the long-gone days. There is a biblical precedent for this as there is for all the other hardships imposed on women – *I will greatly multiply thy sorrow and thy conception; in sorrow thou shalt bring forth children* (Genesis 3:16). ✪ Look at the way that Offred describes childbirth in our society. Is it any better for the women concerned than this natural birth that Gilead prescribes? Again we have the contrast of the old society with Gilead and Offred quite fairly accepts the faults of the old ways. ✪ Why do you think in this chapter there is no memory of Offred's own birth experience?

Offred imagines the Wives chatting about their Handmaids as if they were pet animals or servants, or even daughters. The Wives have very little power in Gilead and so they must exercise it where they can – over the Handmaids and during the births. The doctors (all men of course) are banned from the event just as they were in the times of the early Puritan colony in this town.

Atwood fills in some important details for us in this section, the most important being to set the time for the closure of the Red Centre as a school – the mid-1980s. This gives us a fix on when the present events are taking place.

Chapter 20

◆ Offred goes into the room where Janine, or Ofwarren, will give birth.
◆ She remembers the movies they were shown at the Red Centre.
◆ She remembers her mother in her sixties.

We see another ritual of this strange society – the birthing ritual. The Wives are in one room pretending that Ofwarren's Wife is about to give birth, while all the Handmaids in the area are upstairs in the master bedroom with Ofwarren. Offred remembers another of Aunt Lydia's Bible sayings *From each according to her ability, to each, according to his needs.* Notice the way that gender has been altered in this saying. The irony is of course that this is not a quotation from the Bible about how women who can have babies should provide them for men who are childless, but is in fact from Karl Marx who suggested that in society those who are more able should support those who cannot provide for themselves.

Offred remembers movies they were shown, first at the Red Centre, then from a much earlier time at her high school, when she watched a movie of primitive societies. Aunt Lydia's film is about women protesting in favour of legalized abortion (in the USA abortion was legalized in certain cases in the early 1970s) and against rape (the slogan 'take back the night' was used by feminist groups in a campaign to make the streets safe for women at night). Holding one of the banners is Offred's mother, looking young and wearing the same kind of clothes that Moira would wear.

This memory leads on to another – of her mother, much older but still a feminist, telling the story of how hard it had been to bring up a child as a single parent. (The film would put Offred's mother in her twenties, during the 1960s, before abortion was legalized in the USA. If she was 37 when Offred was born, perhaps 10–15 years after the film, that would mean Offred was born in the early 1970s and going to school with Moira in the late 1980s. We can then guess at the present timeframe which is probably in the early 2000s.) Offred's mother is an old-fashioned isolationist feminist. She wants no truck with men, considering them only useful for making more women, playing football and mending cars. She considers Offred a backlash, a temporary glitch in the movement towards a woman-oriented society where men have little or no role. ✪ Is she right?

Chapter 21

◆ Offred takes part in the birth of Janine's baby.

The customs that Gilead Wives have decided on closely reflect the days of the early settlers when all the women in the area would attend and take part in a birth. For them birth was a dangerous occasion and many women died. Janine is in a slightly less precarious position, although if the baby turns out to be a shredder it might seal her fate. The Ceremony is foolish, with the Wives pretending that the older woman is also giving birth as she sits on a specially made birthing stool above Janine. Ofwarren is a sad figure, abandoned to her own suffering once the birth has taken place. Again Offred is partly caught up in the hysteria of the moment and partly cynical, noting the Wife's fluffy slippers like toilet seat covers but also experiencing ghost labour pains for Janine. Afterwards on the way home she reflects that there are elements in the afternoon's events which her mother would have approved of – a society dominated by women.

Chapter 22

◆ Offred tells the story of Moira's escape.

Moira escapes in true heroine style by tying up one of the Aunts, stealing her clothes and pass and just walking away. Offred hears this story from Janine who is asked by the Aunts to spy on the other Handmaids. Moira's story is told to us by Offred, who repeats Janine's story heard from Aunt Lydia. It is a story within a story within a story, but Offred makes up the important details about Janine's responses and Moira's words to Elizabeth. The response of the other women at the Red Centre is interesting – they both feared the consequences and saw the centre as a refuge. At the same time they loved Moira for her bravery and the thought that she had shown the Aunts to be vulnerable. ○ Why does Atwood tell this story at this stage?

Chapter 23

◆ Offred plays Scrabble with the Commander.

The chapter begins after Offred has visited the Commander and she is going over in her head what has happened and whether she acted in her own best interests. What strikes her first is that she is determined to wait out this life and hope for a better one. Her second thought is that power isn't about who can do what to whom, but rather who can do what to whom and *be forgiven for it.* ○ How do you think this is relevant to the scene that follows – playing Scrabble?

There is another frisson of perverse sexuality as Offred makes her way to the Commander's office where presumably he can do whatever he wants to her, unsanctioned by Serena Joy. At the Ceremony she was bored and sad and angry but now she is really afraid of what might happen to her. At the same time she knows that this is an opening for her. Perhaps she will be able to negotiate with the

Commander for something for herself. The Commander has a special room where women are not allowed, with books and a computer. Only Guardians are allowed in there to clean it. Despite her fear, Offred can mock the Commander's posing at the fireplace, his pathetic attempts to make her feel sorry for him. This man has no reason to be pleasant to Offred; he can make whatever demands he wants and no one will believe her. Instead he asks for things – the Scrabble game, the kiss.

Offred, later in her room, imagines that she could kill him while he is in this vulnerable state, but this is not what she feels at the time. All of his actions, framed in a gentlemanly, almost coy way, are treason, and they could both be destroyed if they were found out. ✪ What is the significance of the game they play? Why Scrabble, not Monopoly or Snakes and Ladders? Do you think the Commander has chosen this game deliberately?

LANGUAGE, STYLE AND STRUCTURE

The excitement of the birth is matched by the excitement of the story of Moira's escape and the description of the community of women delivering the child is set beside stories about her mother, a politically active feminist. The boredom and hopelessness of the earlier parts of the book are temporarily left behind, although Offred's cynicism and humour are still firmly in place. The day starts badly with Offred repeatedly dreaming that she wakes in another reality. Her mood is reflected in the *drowned white hair* of the curtains and the images she associates with the eggshell, *a barren landscape.* Her memories of her mother are good ones. In the movie her mother is a beautiful, independent young woman, much like Moira. Even the quarrelling between her mother and Luke is affectionate rather than aggressive.

Over to you

- ❓ Use Offred's account to write an account of the birth ceremony for the anthropologists of the future.
- ❓ Add to your Mind Map of the Commander. Why has he asked Offred down to his room to play Scrabble?

Do his mild manners and engaging behaviour make him less frightening, or more so?

? Find a quotation from this section of the novel to support the following statements:

1 The Commander remembers the sexual politics of the old days before Gilead.
2 Offred finds the Scrabble game a sensual experience.
3 She is ashamed and angry at herself for enjoying the game and playing along with the Commander.
4 After a few months in the Red Centre the Handmaids were indoctrinated into becoming passive, afraid to fight back.
5 Janine was so damaged by her experiences in life and at the Red Centre that she no longer had any moral sense.
6 Offred often fought with her mother over their different lifestyles.

? Look over the material we have about Offred's mother (draw a Mind Map for her – one is begun for you on the previous page). How does what she says about men and their usefulness compare with the roles of men and women in Gilead? Has the current state justified her beliefs? What might Offred's mother's *utopian* state be like? Would men come to the same harm that women experience in Gilead? You might like to discuss this with someone else and draw up a plan of a separatist feminist utopia.

? What do the following figures of speech refer to? What do you think Atwood means by them?
... like an elevator with open sides
... like enormous haloes, festooned with fruit and flowers, and the feathers of exotic birds
... of raw egg white
... as if I'm a kitten in a window. One he doesn't intend to buy.
... a smell of dens, of inhabited caves
... like a doll, an old one that's been pillaged and discarded in some corner

Take a break. Play a game of Scrabble.

IX Night

Chapter 24

◆ Offred remembers an old television documentary.
◆ She starts to laugh.

Offred returns to her room. She is shocked and relieved by what has just happened to her. The events downstairs with the Commander make her take stock of her life. She admits that until now she had been living in a two-dimensional world, seeing only her immediate surroundings. She decides that she will give up her secret life – her name, her memories – and just live in the present, accepting her life of constriction and control, making the best of what she has

and negotiating with the Commander for some small luxuries.
○ What do you think Offred means when she says *Context is all*? Do you think she will give up her memories and her name?

Having said that she will live in the present, Offred then goes back to her childhood and a television documentary she watched when she was a child, in the 1970s. The documentary is an interview with the mistress of a Nazi concentration camp commander. Offred remembers her mother's admiration for the woman who has kept herself attractive for all those intervening years and she remembers that the woman committed suicide immediately after the interview. ○ Why does Offred dredge up this memory at this stage?

Offred suddenly feels as if she is cracking open. A burst of hysterical laughter builds up inside her. If it is heard it could mean her death. The laughter seems a cathartic experience for her but the chapter concludes with a consideration of the motto scratched on her cupboard floor and Offred decides that even that is worthless as an act of resistance because she has no way of escaping.

LANGUAGE, STYLE AND STRUCTURE

At the beginning of this chapter Atwood gives us graphic images of how Offred sees her two-dimensional life. Her face becomes a map of her life with tiny hairs, veins and skin mapping out the futility. She has used images of her body in earlier sections of the book, where she describes herself as a mist surrounding a womb, or her body has become a fenland where wild animals lurk. Later in this same chapter, when she laughs her body becomes a volcano and begins to crack open, to explode. Her body is all that Offred owns or can make reference to and she observes it as if it were something distinct from herself. Again, she talks about composing herself as if the self that she is now is a construct, no longer the real person.
○ Look at the description of her curtains in this chapter. How is it different from the description in Chapter 19?

Structurally this chapter seems to mark a turning-point for Offred. She has decided to give up her inner life and her memories and live for the future. She admits she will never get out of this situation and she rejects the motto from the previous Handmaid. The memory of the Nazi's mistress puts Offred firmly, she believes, in the role of collaborator, and she accepts it.

Now try this

? What are the parallels between Offred and the Nazi mistress, the Commander and the Nazi, and their situations? In the grid opposite choose which option either woman has and comment in the box provided. The first has been done for you. After you have filled it in, decide if you think Offred is morally any better than the Nazi mistress.

You've earned a break – have a laugh for a while – but don't die laughing!

X Soul Scrolls

Chapter 25

◆ The next morning Cora thinks Offred has killed herself.
◆ Offred describes the passing of spring in the garden.
◆ She recounts more visits to the Commander.

Cora thinks that Offred is dead. *'Like ...'* she begins to say, from which we infer that the previous Handmaid has died in this room. Offred thinks constantly about the means of killing herself but is not yet ready to do so. Taking her own life would be a form of resistance to the state. Cora and Offred are finding things in common. We have already been told that Cora hopes for a child to look after and that she chooses not to disapprove of Offred's role in the house. Now the two conspire together to keep the secret of the lost breakfast from the rest of the house. We can see that a possible life is emerging for Offred in this house, even if it will only last two

	voluntary/ forced relationship	willing/ unwilling participant	knows/ doesn't know about violence	believes/ doesn't believe in the system	feels guilt/ doesn't feel guilt	loves/ doesn't love	close to/ away from violence
Offred (+ Commander)	Offred 'chooses' to become a Handmaid. She could tell Serena Joy about it						
Mistress (+ Nazi)	Freely chooses Nazi as lover – not a captive – could walk away at any time						

years, the duration of her posting there. Her past is receding and she is becoming Offred.

Another complex shift in Offred's various time frames takes place here. In the previous chapter she was telling the story as if it was her immediate present. The time frame was late spring. But now Offred describes the passing of several months and for another two chapters she tells the Gilead story as if it were in the past. ✪ Why does Atwood choose to do this?

There follows a very erotic piece of writing describing the subversive fruitfulness of the garden. Offred's sexual needs, as well as her desire for freedom, are imposed on this garden; the walls seem to soften as she leans on them and the willow whispers secrets. She has relaxed enough to begin to flirt with the Guardian Angels at the checkpoint. ✪ What is the significance of the picture which precedes this of Serena Joy deadheading the finished tulip flowers?

The Scrabble games continue along the same lines and Offred and the Commander work out a system for meeting, always determined by the Commander, of course. On the second night he gives her a magazine from her childhood – a *Vogue*. The magazine reminds Offred of her former life and she asks the Commander why he has caused her this pain. His answer shows the gulf between them. She thinks of the pain she is given by being reminded that once she could make choices, but he thinks about having someone he can share his tastes with. She is not a person with a past to him. When he looks at the picture of the model, Offred thinks it is as if he is looking at an almost extinct animal in a zoo. The conversation ends with the old cliché that the man's wife doesn't understand him. If Offred didn't understand what the Commander wanted before, she does now – a mistress.

✪ Offred sees the pictures of the women in the magazine as if they were pirates, or cats about to pounce. They are images of freedom and power. What would Offred's mother have made of those models and the articles in the magazine? Which of them would be right?

On the third meeting Offred asks for hand cream. The Commander is quite naturally and unconsciously patronizing towards her – he is amused that the Handmaids are clever enough to think of using butter to soften their skin.

His replies to Offred make her realize that he has had other mistresses, even before the rise of Gilead, because he is aware of what will make Serena Joy suspicious. He seems to enjoy the subterfuge. Like the Nazi leaders who planned the Holocaust but never witnessed its implementation, he has no idea of the details of the Handmaids' lives. He can even tolerate Offred's anger at him when she tells him what her room would be searched for. He is so powerful that her anger cannot touch him. She is just an animal in a cage to him.

Chapter 26

◆ The next Ceremony takes place.
◆ Offred thinks about how her feelings about both Serena Joy and the Commander have changed.

A month has passed since Offred began going to the Commander's office. The next Ceremony is embarrassing to her; she thinks about how unfeminine she is now with body hair and no cosmetics. The Commander absent-mindedly puts his hand up to her face, an act which could get Offred killed if Serena Joy noticed it. She also feels guilty, as if she has taken something from Serena Joy, and jealous of Serena Joy's claims on the Commander.

Offred thinks briefly about Aunt Lydia's plans for the future. One day, when the population has increased enough, the Handmaids can become part of the household and not be transferred from house to house. Their daughters, some of whom will presumably become the next generation of Handmaids, will have more rights, even their own garden.

Relations between Offred and the Commander have changed. She has become like his mistress, speaking her mind, angling for small luxuries, even talking quite sharply to him, but all the time aware that he has total power over her.

Chapter 27

◆ Offred remembers ice cream parlours.
◆ She and Ofglen are shopping. They go to the Wall and to Soul Scrolls.
◆ They make contact for the first time.

It is midsummer and Offred remembers what things used to be like. For all her determination not to live in the past she still does so. She remembers taking her daughter for an ice cream, wearing a summer dress and sandals instead of the enveloping red habit. Offred also thinks about Luke, how she still imagines that he is inside the Wall in the old university campus which is now the headquarters of the Eyes.

They stop outside what must be the strangest example of Gilead society so far. Inside computers are printing out and then recycling prayers. Why would Gilead waste its limited resources on this? ❷ Is this any sillier or worse than the practice among some Catholic communities of paying the local priest to say prayers for the repose of someone's soul? It is still a custom in some Catholic communities to buy a certificate from a holy order guaranteeing that a dead person's soul will be prayed for every day, *ad infinitum*.

In the reflection of the window Ofglen and Offred meet each others eyes. Ofglen utters a blasphemy and Offred repeats it. The two have become conspirators. Ofglen tells Offred that there are more people, a subversive organization. Offred's first thought is to ask for news about Luke and her daughter. While they talk a black van stops beside them and takes a passer-by. Offred is relieved that it is not her.

Chapter 28

◆ Offred remembers an argument with Moira before she married Luke.
◆ She looks back to the start of the Gilead regime.
◆ She remembers losing her job and her bank account.
◆ She remembers a much earlier time in the 1970s when her mother was hurt in a demonstration.
◆ Her relationship with Luke was changed by the new state.

Much of the detective work we have been doing as we read the novel is rounded out in this chapter. Offred's argument with Moira shows the distinction between Moira's feminism and that of Offred's mother. Moira has chosen to become a lesbian. She believes that Offred can have relationships with men, but that she should not engage in a relationship with someone who is married. ❷ What would Offred's mother have said?

💔 Offred's job had been in a library transferring books on to computer discs. By this time there was no paper money, everything was paid for with plastic cards, a logical outcome of events when Atwood was writing this book in 1985. Much of this has already come about – lots of library archives are now only accessible on disc and very few people use regular money for any large transaction.

👫 The regime now in power kills the entire cabinet and makes it look like a terrorist attack. The constitution is suspended and the media is stifled. Few people protest because all the actions of those who take power seem reasonable enough in a national emergency. People even approved of some of the early measures – introducing identipasses, closing down pornography shops, Feels on Wheels vans and the like. Then Offred tells her own version of the events around which all women were removed from the workforce, and their bank accounts were terminated. A new army appears on the streets. The people who protest are shot at. ❂ Is this credible? Could a huge, powerful state like the USA be transformed so quickly and effortlessly as Atwood suggests? Look at the history of the Third Reich and compare the position of women in this new state with the Jews in Germany.

Offred goes back in time to an earlier memory of her mother coming home after a demonstration. She and her mother both felt they had failed to live up to the other's expectations. Offred's mother had failed to give her the stability and mothering that she needed and Offred had failed to appreciate or live out her mother's politics. ❂ Would Offred's mother have approved of Moira?

💔 Offred recounts how she was affected by the loss of her job and bank account in more than just a physical way. It affected her feelings of independence and freedom. She could no longer see her husband as an equal but now had to be dependent on him. She is too afraid to mention this to him because now she is utterly dependent on him for her survival.

Chapter 29

◆ Offred asks the Commander what *Nolite te bastardes carborundum* means.

◆ She realizes that the last Handmaid visited the Commander too.

◆ Finally she feels she has some control over him and asks for information.

A considerable amount of time must have passed, since Offred has read two novels and lots of magazines. The Commander seems content to play Scrabble and watch her read. When they talk he tells her that he is a sort of scientist. ✪ What do you think he means by this? Is this statement more or less frightening than if he explained in detail what he did? His attitude is still patronizing in the extreme. Offred still feels as if she is a caged animal that he enjoys watching. Worse still she learns that he has brought her into his study even though the last Handmaid died as a result of their meetings. ✪ What does this tell you about how he regards Offred? Offred has been asking herself why the Commander brings her down here and now she feels she knows – her enjoyment of the times in his office justify the state that he has helped create, and makes him feel he is a compassionate man. Now that she knows he feels guilty about what he is doing, she asks him for information.

LANGUAGE, STYLE AND STRUCTURE

The tone of Offred's narrative has changed a great deal in this section of the novel. The earlier emotionally wrought memories forced out of Offred have given way to a calmer, more melancholy set of memories. There are fewer outbursts of metaphors and her memories are structured. She has decided to recall the events surrounding the coup which ended the USA and even though it is told through her own experience the story is coherent and complete. Two passages in this section describe the garden as a place of desire where, despite Serena Joy's efforts to control (and castrate), the flowers and wildlife are a riot of colour and sensuality. Later in Chapter 28 she watches Nick in the garden, the bare flesh of his arm mixed in with her sensual awareness of the smells of the plants. This time though the smells have become a *stink*, the flowers are *pulpy growth*, the pollen is like *oyster spawn thrown into the sea*, as if the desire she feels for him repels her.

Organizing your thoughts

? Since 1985 when this novel was written there have been many changes in Western society which Atwood could not have foreseen: CCTV cameras, the Internet, girls becoming higher achievers than boys in school, and women catching up in terms of salary and job prospects. Atwood's earthquakes and the fall in population have not happened. Discuss with a fellow student whether Atwood's cautionary tale is still relevant. Has the threat of a right-wing backlash against women gone forever? Try brainstorming possible scenarios where this might happen.

Before you go on to the next section put your feet up for a while. Borrow your boyfriend/brother's copy of Loaded magazine.

XI Night

Chapter 30

◆ Offred watches Nick cross the lawn.
◆ She remembers Luke killing their cat.
◆ She prays.

Offred looks out over the night garden, affected by her own desires and the heat and passion wafting up from the garden. Nick crosses the lawn and their eyes meet. Offred feels guilty at her desire for Nick when she has no idea what has happened to Luke.

Seeing Nick triggers another memory, of Luke killing their cat just before they left. Her feelings of guilt and betrayal have triggered this memory. Luke kills part of their love just as Offred thinks she is denying Luke's survival by wanting Nick. She blames both things on the state. Offred's memories of her past are becoming less and less clear as she engages more and more in this new life. Offred seems at a very low point in her room alone and on the verge of 'knowing'. She prays for knowledge and understanding but at the same time she fears it and thinks about suicide.

A little bit of work to do

? Offred misquotes two prayers in this section. Do you know what they are? The last prayer, the Lord's Prayer, used to be known to every school student in Britain because it was said every day. It is less well known now. If you don't know the Lord's Prayer, find a copy and write each of its lines beside the relevant part of Offred's prayer. Does she distort its meaning? If so, how and why?

XII Jezebel's

Chapter 31

◆ Offred talks to Ofglen.
◆ Serena Joy suggests that they use Nick to make Offred pregnant.

Where once Offred was overcome with pleasure at the thought of there being a resistance movement, now their secret passwords and networking seem foolish and purposeless. Offred has stopped feeling angry at what has happened to her and now she feels old and tired; even the bodies on the Wall don't seem to affect her. They remind her of how all the Jews in America were allowed to emigrate or convert to Christianity.

Serena Joy proposes to Offred that they should use Nick to make Offred pregnant. The two women have finally found some common goal but for very different motives.

Offred needs a baby so she will not be sent to the Colonies. Serena Joy wants a baby in order to be rid of Offred and others like her, and for other reasons. The two women agree that the Commander shouldn't know about it. Offred is now conspiring with Ofglen, with the Commander, with his wife and, in their secret glances, with Nick. She has settled into this new life and entered the power games that these people play, negotiating for better conditions.

Chapter 32

◆ Offred talks to Rita.
◆ She considers using the match to kill herself.
◆ She recalls the Commander, a little drunk, asking her what she thinks of Gilead.

Whereas once talking to Rita would have been an act of subversion, a cheat against their rules, now it is far less significant. Rita has accepted Offred as a part of the daily routine and Offred is now only cynical about Rita's gesture in giving her an ice cube. Rita too, Offred thinks, is on the make, wants something from her: *Have I become, suddenly, one of those who must be appeased?*

Offred hurries upstairs to smoke her cigarette but decides not to. The match is a possible weapon of rebellion. She could use it to kill herself and take the Commander and his household with her.

We hear a little justification from the Commander for the state he has helped create. The sexual freedom and equality that women experienced in the late 1980s led to dissatisfaction among men, he tells Offred. Sex was freely available and so was no longer a prize to be fought for and controlled. Now, he says, men are happier even though they have less access to women and sex, because now they value what is in short supply. He knows what Offred thinks of the state he has created and recognizes that some people have been harmed by the new system but feels, just the same, justified.

Back in her room Offred's thoughts no longer turn to her lost family but to the women downstairs in the kitchen with whom she might become friends. Her other thoughts are of suicide.

Chapter 33

◆ Offred goes to a Prayvaganza.
◆ She sees Janine and remembers a story about her from the Red Centre.

The local community is holding a Prayvaganza and, although Offred does not tell us what it will be, we can imagine. This society seems to thrive on pageant and ritual and Offred points out the pattern of pairs of Handmaids, like Dutch dolls on wallpaper, moving towards the hall. The Wives and daughters are seated on one side of a courtyard and the Handmaids kneel on the other side. In a gallery are the other ranks of women, who attend out of choice. Ofglen tells her that Janine's baby turned out to be a shredder, deformed in some way, and she can see that Janine is in ill health. Offred remembers Janine on the verge of insanity at the Red Centre, and how she was brought back only by a slap and some harsh talking from Moira.

Chapter 34

◆ Offred watches a marriage ceremony.
◆ She recalls more of the Commander's justification for the state of Gilead.
◆ She remembers Moira.

The ceremony where daughters, some of them 14 years old, are given to Angels is counterpointed with Offred's memory of the Commander explaining what was wrong with the system of finding marriage partners in the time before. ◗ Can you find any fault in what the Commander says? When he asks Offred what is missing from the new system she answers, 'Love.' If he asked you, is this what you would say? Not freedom of choice, democracy, human rights, freedom from slavery – but love?

As she watches these innocent young girls being paired off with complete strangers Offred is at her most cynical. She imagines the failure and disappointment of these young men and women when they are actually alone together. Her memory of Moira's whispered obscenities makes her more cheerful and confirms that in her present state this is the most healthy attitude she can take. As they leave, Ofglen asks her to find out information for the underground movement in her meetings with the Commander. ✪ How do you think Ofglen found out?

Chapter 35

◆ Offred remembers the checkpoint on the border with Canada.
◆ She remembers what falling in love was like.
◆ Serena Joy produces a photograph of Offred's daughter.

Offred fluctuates between her feeling that resistance is futile and her angry, cynical but silent fighting back against the system. Alone and waiting again in her room, she segues from the idea of herself as an invalid, brought food on a tray, to the other use of the word *invalid*, which reminds her of the moment when she and Luke were caught with fake passports. Abruptly she pushes the memory away and decides she will think instead about love. ✪ Reading her version of the way things were before, does it sound any more attractive than the Commander's version in Chapter 34? She describes murders, loss, change, blame. Thinking that Luke might not have been her final partner, she comes back to the guilty feelings about how long she must go on mourning for him. War widows are given closure but Offred has none.

Serena Joy shows Offred a photo, supposedly of Offred's daughter. Instead of feeling happiness that her daughter is alive and well, Offred feels desolate and abandoned.

Chapter 36

◆ The Commander takes Offred out.

We are back in the immediate present, presumably the night after Offred has attended the Prayvaganza and has seen her daughter's photograph. The Commander gives Offred a cheap, tatty dress and she feels a mixture of disgust and attraction. ✪ Would Offred have agreed to wear this garment in the old days, with Luke or some earlier partner? What would her mother say about it? What would Moira say? The thought of how horrified the Aunts would be drives her to put it on and she feels a thrill of excitement even while she wonders what kinky sex the Commander is about to propose. They get in the car, and arrive at a place that the

Commander has been to before. It is obvious that he has carefully planned this adventure. ✪ Why would he take these risks?

Chapter 37

◆ The Commander shows off in the brothel.
◆ Offred sees Moira.

Offred is amazed to see the glittering array of women, all apparently flouting every rule about female conduct in Gilead. ✪ Is this brothel a place of freedom or control for these women? Is it better than the Colonies? Here we have a patriarchal system operating at its most functional level. Women have become a resource in this society. Men in the lower ranks must work hard and please the Commanders in order to be given access to the national resource, whether it be a Wife or a Handmaid. Here, at the highest level, the Commanders treat themselves to unlimited quantities of the national resource. Female flesh is on show, and the Commanders can choose whichever woman they want, whether it is sex in one of the bedrooms or a chat with the lawyer turned prostitute.

The Commander's attitude is strange. He is cheating the system which he created, both by sanctioning the existence of this place but also by bringing Offred here in secret. The other Commanders don't do this; it breaks their rules. This seems to be the Commander's element of resistance to the state. Like a teenage boy he is showing off in front of Offred.

Offred doesn't recognize it but Moira is wearing a shabby Bunny Girl outfit, the costume once worn by the waitresses at a famous chain of nightclubs. ✪ What is the irony in Moira being dressed in this shabby version of a once famous male plaything?

Chapter 38

◆ Moira tells her story.

Moira's story is exciting and tells us much about how things worked out in Gilead after Offred went to the Red

Centre. We know now that Luke and Offred had been made into criminals because of his divorce. We learn more details about the Colonies and who goes there. But Moira has been broken by the system. In the previous chapter we saw Offred consigning Luke to her past and then seeing her daughter living on happily without her. Now another remnant of her past, Moira is here, abused and made accepting by what has happened to her.

Chapter 39

◆ Offred and the Commander go up to a room.
◆ She flashes back to Moira's story about seeing her mother.

💔 Finally, a key figure from her past life is accounted for. Her mother disappeared while she and Luke were still together and Moira has seen her in a movie about the Colonies. She is almost certainly now dead or dying, also broken by the state. There follows an even more painfully sad sex scene where Offred is probably at her lowest ebb. All the people she loved are disposed of now; she can hold no more illusions about ever being back with them. She is dressed in a tawdry outfit in a hotel room with a fascist who pretends to be kindly. It is worse for her than if Serena Joy were there.

Your turn

? Look back to the Mind Maps you have created for each of the characters and add the most recent events to them. You could also add to the information you have collected about the state of Gilead, the list of newly coined words and the comparison between the Commander and the Nazi concentration camp commandant.

? Do you agree with Moira's view of the Commander? What would she say about the following:

Nick
Offred conspiring with Serena Joy
Offred's dreams of escape
The Prayvaganzas
Offred's thoughts of suicide

? In the few months she has been at the Commander's house we have been shown a number of relationships. Match up these pairs of characters with the word or words below which best illustrate them.

Offred and the Commander
Offred and Serena Joy
Offred and Nick
Offred and Luke
Offred and Moira
Offred and her mother
The Commander and Serena Joy
Nick and the Commander

calculating, cold, affectionate, passionless, self-interested, tender, scheming, exploitative, loving, kindly, patronizing

Can you think of any other words which should be added here?

XIII Night

*C*hapter 40

◆ Offred visits Nick.

Offred gives us two accounts of her meeting with Nick, both of which she says are false. One is romantic in the old sense of falling into a passionate embrace, while the other is set in the style of an old movie where the participants wisecrack with one another. Whichever version is closest to the truth, Offred is ashamed of how her body has responded to this man when she doesn't even know whether Luke is dead or alive.

LANGUAGE, STYLE AND STRUCTURE

Previous 'Night' sections have been passages of relived memories while Offred is passively waiting for the next day. Now, though, the night is taken up with her new passion for life. It marks a transition in the novel where Offred has finally abandoned all her hopes for the past to be reinstated.

XIV Salvaging

Chapter 41

◆ Offred describes how her desire for Nick grows.
◆ Ofglen suggests that Offred should spy on the Commander.

Offred seems to be feeling the way she has already described people who fall in love. She knows little or nothing about Nick but her physical passion for him dominates everything else in her life: her memories, her sense of resistance to the state, Ofglen's whisperings, and especially the Commander. Now that she has Nick, she has to force herself to be interested in the older man.

Chapter 42

◆ Offred watches a Handmaid executed.

A similar event to the Prayvaganza but with a little more pomp. Offred tries to think what this Handmaid might have done. She tells us that the punishment for reading is amputation of a hand, so it must be something worse. ✪ Why have the authorities stopped telling the public what crimes have been committed?

Chapter 43

◆ Offred takes part in a Particicution.

The latent violence of this state is finally laid out before us. Until now there have been suggestions and hints but the whole business of punishment has been sanctified and sanitized by law. Now we watch as a crowd of Handmaids are whipped up into such a frenzy that they kill a man with their bare hands. The event finally sees an end to poor Janine's sanity. We see her wandering about with a hank of hair in her hand. The Wives and daughters are free to leave while this is happening. ✪ Why do you think many of them stay to watch?

The Guardian is no rapist but is in fact a member of Ofglen's underground who has been discovered. Why would the state want to execute him in this way? Ofglen risks her own life to knock him out before he is torn to pieces. It is all she can do to help him and is an act of great bravery.

Chapter 44

◆ Ofglen has killed herself.

Offred has become completely engrossed in her new life, enjoying her lunch, looking forward to shopping with Ofglen, catching glimpses of Nick in the garden. The horror of the morning has gone. But when she goes outside there is a new Ofglen, one who is not part of the underground and who warns Offred off when she uses the password. Ofglen has given herself away at the Salvaging and has committed suicide as the secret police have come for her so as not to give away any of her co-conspirators. Offred is thrown back into the mental anguish of the first few chapters. All the comforts she has built up around her have crashed down around her ears. She hopes that Ofglen's suicide has saved her.

Chapter 45

◆ Serena Joy has found the cloak and dress.

In her panic Offred makes bargains with the unknown offering everything, even Nick, if she can avoid the pain of torture and hanging. Here she is like Winston Smith, the protagonist of Orwell's *1984*, shouting out that he wants Julia fed to the rats not himself. For the first time she says she truly feels the power that this state has over her.

When Serena Joy accuses Offred of betraying her trust, Offred has no idea what she has found out; there have been so many betrayals. Offred can only keep silent and wait to find out what Serena Joy knows. It turns out that the embittered wife has found the cloak and dress. ❂What will she do next? If she denounces Offred what will happen to her husband?

XV Night

Chapter 46 Six

◆ Offred waits.
◆ Eyes come for her.

Offred is calm as she sits and waits for Serena Joy's punishment. She considers suicide by using her match or by knotting a bedsheet and hanging herself. She thinks of walking down the street until she is arrested, or going to the Commander to beg for his help, or fleeing to Nick. But she does nothing. An image comes to her of the previous Offred dangling from the light fitting in the dress that Offred wore to Jezebel's. The memory of the other woman tells her to get on with it, but as she gets up to kill herself the black van comes to the house.

When the men come to her room Nick is with them. He promises her safety if she goes with the Eyes. On the way downstairs the Commander and Serena Joy look amazed and vulnerable. Neither of them has had any part in Offred's arrest. The Commander even tries to stop them taking her. Cora weeps for the lost child that Offred may be carrying.

Historical Notes

◆ A century and a half later a symposium investigates the tapes containing Offred's story.
◆ The chief topic is the identity of the Commander.
◆ The speaker speculates on Offred's ultimate fate.

Unlike the heroine of the movie based on the novel, Offred doesn't murder the Commander and run off to a trailer in Canada. That she made the tapes tells us that the Eyes that came for her were probably members of the Mayday underground and that she spent some time at least at liberty. The regime has long ended and is an object for historical research. Some things, however, never change: Dr Pieixoto is pompous and patronizing, making sexist jokes about the derivation of words.

All through the novel, Offred, in her role as narrator, has reminded us that this is a story that she is constructing – her shifts in time both from the point of view of narration and back and forth in memory make this a complex narrative to interpret. Moira's story is largely made up by Offred and so are the conversations between the Wives and the encounters that she imagines between the daughters and Angels. Here we realize that this story is not only a construction on Offred's part but is also a construct of the anthropologists who discovered and transcribed the tapes. It is interesting to note that Atwood gives the story's naming to Pieixoto, the feeble pun-maker who draws parallels between Offred's story and the stories of the Canterbury Tales. ✪ Do you think there are parallels between this story and Chaucer's?

Over to you

? The job of the anthropologists who had Offred's tapes was to find out as much as they could about Gilead, not about Offred. Using their own techniques, what can you infer about the society that holds the conference? Write an anthropologist's report on the newly discovered minutes of the twelfth Symposium on Gileadean Studies, discovered hundreds of years after the University of Denay had disappeared.

? At several crucial points in the story of Offred, the movie and the novel diverge. Why do you think the movie makers changed the following:

Moira's escape and Offred's part in it
Luke's death
Offred's removal from the Commander's house
Janine's Birth Day
The wedding ceremony
Offred's mother
Offred and Moira's past
Jezebel's
The ceremony and what Offred does afterwards

Find some other areas where the movie has altered the characters and say what effect it has on the themes of the novel.

CRITICAL APPROACHES

The Handmaid's Tale has been viewed by critics from the perspective of the science fiction genre, where it joins a whole series of feminist utopia/dystopia novels such as Ursula Le Guin's *The Dispossessed* or Marge Piercy's *Woman on the Edge of Time*. It can also be seen within the context of novels, such as George Orwell's *1984*, in which the writer takes aspects of their own society and develops them to an extreme form. Both genres engage the reader with aspects of their own society and teach them about the nature of that society or their existence. The novel can also be viewed as an examination of women's space in history, developing the idea of 'herstory' as opposed to 'history'.

Patrick D. Murphy (1990) suggests that the novel is a 'parable about ourselves', linking it with other dystopian novels which draw out ideas about our own society by creating imaginary future ones. Murphy takes this idea a stage further by suggesting that unlike other dystopian novels, which have a kind of closure to them, *The Handmaid's Tale* breaks off Offred's tale, leaving the reader dissatisfied, at a loss. He says that instead of turning our concerns into a satisfying shape, as the novel might do if Offred killed the Commander and ran off to the mountains, it makes uncomfortable reading, making us aware of our circumstances and encouraging us to effect political change or at least to be aware of the possibilities for change. The power of the novel, he says, is its ability to provoke action rather than relieve anxiety. We come away from it feeling as if the issues it has brought to the surface are still unresolved, that we must act in some way to resolve them. It is in many ways a cautionary tale, warning us that all the gains made in women's lives could be lost in one reactionary political change.

Other critics view the novel through the perspective of the Scrabble game. Madonne Miner (1991) suggests that the game gives us a clue to the basic contradictions in Offred's narrative.

In the novel the game is forbidden – Offred is not allowed to read or write and there is a feeling that with the letters of the Scrabble board any kind of subversion is possible. The game is so forbidden that the Commander does not even play it with his Wife and it is a kind of adultery that he plays it with Offred. But normal Scrabble has clear rules about what can be done with the letters. Despite this, Offred and the Commander break the rules, make up nonsense words, and take more letters than they are allowed. The fact that Offred willingly breaks the rules suggests to Madonne Miner that she can break other rules too, such as those connected with her story. We see this in the two different and untruthful versions of her meeting with Nick and in the made-up stories she tells us about the Wives and about Moira's escape. Miner suggests that on the strength of these we cannot trust Offred's narrative, particularly the way in which she is redeemed by her love for Nick. Rather than being redeemed by him she is trapped by him in the Commander's house and seduced away from her other alternatives – suicide or the Mayday organization.

Coral Ann Howells (1995) suggests that the significant feature of the novel within its sci-fi context is its perspective on feminism and power. The many voices of the feminist movement, from the 1960s to the present post-feminist attitudes, are represented in the novel by the many women who populate it, even those who wish to see women back in the home. Atwood points out the word 'feminist' can mean anything, from people who think women should be taught to read, to those who propose separatist lifestyles or suggest that men are redundant. Howells sees the novel as Atwood's rejection of the slogans and binary oppositions of some feminist attitudes. Offred's multiple vision survives Gilead, even if only in her tapes, long after the other women with their extreme attitudes have gone. Again, Howells believes it is Offred's storytelling which is the focus of the novel: *Because I'm telling you this story, I will your existence. I tell, therefore you are.* She sees the romance plot as a redeeming one and the ambiguities of the storytelling as Offred's inability to express the depth of her feelings.

Some critics take the epigraph from Swift as the key to understanding the novel. By using it, Atwood is telling us from the start that this is a satire, not to be taken too seriously. Others have pointed out the Gothic nature of the plot, as well as the unexpected romance which develops towards the end of Offred's story, and the sado-masochistic, voyeuristic elements which we read uncomfortably expecting the worst for Offred at every turn. For others it is the Oedipal nature of Offred's betrayal of Serena Joy that informs the novel.

Atwood herself has talked extensively about the novel and has asserted many times that there is nothing in Gilead that hasn't already existed or been perpetrated already in some state or other. As Offred herself points out, Gilead's only genius is its ability to adapt what has gone before.

SOURCES

Coral Ann Howells, 'Science Fiction in the Feminine', in *Margaret Atwood*, St Martin's Press, New York, 1995.

Madonne Miner, '"Trust me": Reading The Romance Plot in Margaret Atwood's "The Handmaid's Tale"', *20th Century Literature*, 37 (1991).

Patrick D. Murphy, 'Reducing the Dystopian Distance: Pseudo-documentary Framing Future Fiction', *Science Fiction Studies*, 17 (1990).

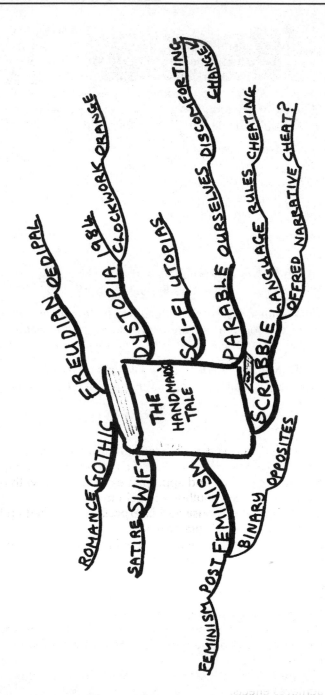

In *all your study, in coursework, and in exams, be aware of the following:*

- **Characterization** – the characters and how we know about them (e.g. speech, actions, author description), their relationships, and how they develop.
- **Plot and structure** – story and how it is organized into parts or episodes.
- **Setting and atmosphere** – the changing physical scene and how it reflects the story (e.g. a storm reflecting chaos).
- **Style and language** – the author's choice of words, and literary devices such as imagery, and how these reflect the **mood**.
- **Viewpoint** – how the story is told (e.g. through an imaginary narrator, or in the third person but through the eyes of one character – 'She was furious – how dare he!').
- **Social and historical context** – the author's influences (see 'Context').
- **Critical approaches** – different ways in which the text has been, or could be, interpreted.

Develop *your ability to:*

- Relate **detail** to **broader content, meaning and style**.
- Show understanding of the author's **intentions, technique and meaning** (brief and appropriate comparisons with other works by the same author will gain marks).
- Give **personal response and interpretation**, backed up by **examples** and short **quotations**.
- **Evaluate** the author's achievement (how far does she/he succeed – give reasons).

Make *sure you:*

- Use **paragraphs** and **sentences** correctly.
- Write in an appropriate **register** – formal but not stilted.
- Use short, appropriate quotations as **evidence** of your understanding.
- Use **literary terms** correctly to explain how an author achieves effects.

93

THE EXAM ESSAY

Planning

You will probably have about 45 minutes for one essay. It is worth spending 5–10 minutes planning it. An excellent way to do this is in the three stages below.

1 **Mind Map** your ideas, without worrying about their order yet.
2 **Order** the relevant ideas (the ones that really relate to the question) by numbering them in the order in which you will write the essay.
3 **Gather** your evidence and short quotes.

You could remember this as the **MOG** technique.

Writing and checking

Then write the essay, allowing five minutes at the end for checking relevance, spelling, grammar and punctuation.

Remember!

Stick to the question and always **back up** your points with evidence in the form of examples and short quotations. Note: you can use '…' for unimportant words missed out in a quotation.

Model answer and plan

The next (and final) chapter consists of an answer to an exam question on *The Handmaid's Tale*, with the Mind Map and plan used to write it. Don't be put off if you think you couldn't write an essay like this yet. You'll develop your skills if you work at them. Even if you're reading this the night before the exam, you can easily memorize the MOG technique in order to do your personal best.

The model answer and plan are good examples to follow, but don't learn them by heart. It's better to pay close attention to the wording of the question you choose to answer, and allow Mind Mapping to help you to think creatively and structurally. Before reading the answer, you might like to do a plan of your own to compare with the example. The numbered points, with comments at the end, show why it's a good answer.

MODEL ANSWER AND ESSAY PLAN

QUESTION

There is something powerful in the whispering of obscenities .... about those in power ... It's like a spell, of sorts. It deflates them, reduces them to the common denominator where they can be dealt with. How far do you agree that Offred uses language and storytelling as an act of rebellion against the state?

PLAN

- General response to the question showing understanding of its terms.
- Acknowledge the force of the statement and explain to what extent you agree.
- Overview of the importance of language to the state of Gilead.
- Show ways in which Offred uses language.
- Critics suggest we can't trust Offred's storytelling.
- Conclusion: Offred's story survives where the state of Gilead disappears.

ESSAY

Offred says these words to herself while she watches the weddings at the Prayvaganza. Here she is at her least free – forced to kneel on a stone floor, an unidentifiable figure in a crowd of women just the same as herself. She remembers Moira's obscenities about Aunt Lydia at the Red Centre and tells herself a comforting story about how all these marriages will fail miserably for want of love. Both Moira and Offred have learned the power of language to reduce their tormentors to something that can be dealt with, and we see Offred doing just this many times in the novel.[1]

Many people use language and storytelling for their own ends in this novel: the state as a way of controlling its citizens, the Handmaids as a way of maintaining a sense of identity. Even the Commander in his own way undermines the rules of society with his forbidden Scrabble game.[2] Offred, however,

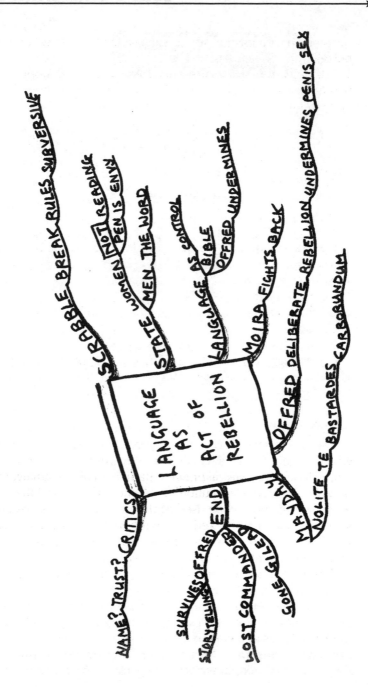

uses her skills for an additional purpose: she retells herself in her story, recreating the person she used to be and reclaiming herself from Gilead.[3]

It is obvious from our first encounters with the dystopian, patriarchal state of Gilead that the men who run it know the power of the word. Women are forbidden to read or write and those caught in the act have their hands cut off. The state uses stories from the Bible to control its citizens and to justify its actions. However, since the Word of God is a powerful weapon, the Bible is locked up and only men have access. At the Prayvaganza the commander in charge of the meeting reads out a long passage taken directly from Timothy, defining the role of women in the righteous state: 'Let women learn in silence with all subjection … but suffer not a woman to teach nor to usurp authority over the man, but to be in silence …'. The message of the state is that language is power and it is not to be used by women.[4]

Offred is aware that the stories she is told at the Rachel and Leah Centre have been carefully selected, and she even catches Lydia out in some deliberate misquotations; 'from each, says the slogan, according to her ability; to each according to his needs.' The Handmaids recite what they think is from St Paul three times each day, but the irony of course is that it is a misquotation from Marx.[5] On another occasion Offred corrects Lydia silently when she misquotes 'all flesh is weak' rather than 'all flesh is grass', a very different meaning.

The state began its career by using the language of advertising to persuade its citizens. Thus we have the new words like 'Prayvaganza' or even 'particicution', an amalgam of 'participate' and 'execution'. Later the state realized that even these words can be used against it and so the tokens and shop signs are now marked only with symbols. One assumes that later no women will be able to read and so the written word will be unnecessary in public places.[6]

There are many examples in this novel of people using talk or storytelling to subvert the state. Moira's obscene outburst against Lydia in Chapter 34 is just one of them. The Marthas' gossip is also a form of resistance. They know they would be punished for such chatter but the gossip is a way of maintaining their old way of life, refusing to abandon what they once were. The Handmaids also use a network of whispering to maintain their old lives. In crowds and at noisy meetings they use the opportunity to exchange names and news. The Mayday resistance movement operates in the same way, actively opposing the state by functioning as an information-gathering operation. The previous Offred, even through death, leaves a message of rebellion against the state: 'Nolite te bastardes carborundum'.

Even the Commander with his illicit games of Scrabble is aware of the power of words to subvert. When he goes as far as offering Offred a pen she remembers the slogan from the Red Centre 'Pen is Envy'. This is a corruption of the Freudian term, but also an acknowledgement by the Aunts of the power of language and of women's desire for it. Offred imagines she can feel the power in the pen as she holds it and tries to recall how to use it.[7]

Offred is conscious of how she can use language to undermine the power of the state to intimidate her. She conjures up obscene images of her oppressors ('his extra, sensitive thumb, his tentacle, his delicate stalked slug's eye, which extrudes, expands, winces, and shrivels back into himself when touched wrongly …').[8] But she also uses language for a far more personal reason. When we first meet Offred she is a jumble of fragmented images which make little sense to us. Gradually, however, she uses her storytelling to reconstruct herself in her own eyes. Her flashbacks gradually grow longer as she deliberately moves into her private space to put the broken pieces of her life back together. As she recounts each episode in her life she is able to put it to rest, finally saying goodbye to Moira, to her mother, to Luke when she commits herself to Nick, and to her daughter when she sees the photograph of her. Offred tells herself into her new life.[9] Offred is aware of the process she is undertaking and constantly considers her storytelling, speaking directly to her listener about the nature of what she is doing:

> I'm sorry there's so much pain in this story. I'm sorry it's in fragments, like a body caught in a crossfire or pulled apart by force. But there is nothing I can do to change it. … By telling you anything at all I'm at least believing in you, I believe you're there, I believe you into existence.[10]

The critic Madonne Miner, in her article '"Trust me": Reading the Romance Plot in Margaret Atwood's "The Handmaid's Tale"', suggests that we cannot trust Offred's storytelling. In the game of Scrabble, Offred and the Commander break the rules associated with the game. Miner sees this as a framework for viewing the novel: she feels that the message Offred gives us, particularly in her relations with Nick, is compromised by the events of the novel. Offred gives up her past and falls in love with Nick. She is unable to describe the scene to us, perhaps because she is aware that it is not the love scene she wants it to be so she makes up two different versions of what happens. She describes herself as a woman in love and herself admits that she can hardly believe the story. The Eyes come for her and Nick's only words are 'Trust me.' But there is no trust in this novel and we never find out if Nick has betrayed her or not.[11]

We should also be aware that Offred tells us her story but never trusts us with her own name. Critics have suggested that her name is there in the text for anyone who can read it – June, the last in her list of names in Chapter 1. It is perhaps Offred's own recognition of the power of words that she keeps her name to herself as she reconstructs her identity.

So, while Offred is aware of the power of language to persuade, to undermine and to confuse I think her chief aim in this novel is a selfish one: she tells her story to reconstruct herself; her subversion of the state is a secondary function. Despite this, it is important to realize that at the end it is Offred's story that survives and not Gilead. Long after Gilead is a historical aberration Offred's story survives, despite the efforts of Pieixoto to reduce its worth.[12]

WHAT EARNED THE MARKS?

1 Acknowledge force of statement.
2 Extends the idea of power over language to the state.
3 Extends the idea of Offred using language as rebellion to storytelling as means of survival.
4 Refers to main themes of novel and illustrates connection between themes and the essay title – the power of language.
5 Gives examples of the way that the state controls language.

6 More examples of the state use of language to control.

7 Examples of language as subversion. Establishes agreement with essay question.

8 Offred using language to subvert and undermine the state – agrees with essay question.

9 Extends the essay title to a further function of Offred's use of storytelling.

10 Examples of the way that Offred is aware of the storytelling process.

11 Refers to critic to suggest the ambiguity of Offred's storytelling process.

12 Concludes by agreeing with title but pointing out that the storytelling process is far more complex process than just subversion.

GLOSSARY OF LITERARY TERMS

aesthetic   concerned with appropriate taste, sensitive to good taste.

alliteration   the repetition, for effect, of consonant sounds at the beginning of words or syllables.

allusion   the use of literary, cultural and historical references.

assonance   the repetition, for effect, of vowel sounds.

caricature   exaggeration and simplification of character traits.

characterization   the way characters are presented, not the characters themselves.

context   the background of social, historical and literary influences on a work.

dialect   regional form of language varying from the standard in vocabulary and grammar.

diction   choice and arrangement of words.

didactic   intended to instruct; in literary criticism, often used in negative sense.

discursive   presenting a logical argument, step by step.

epistolary novel   genre of fiction in which the plot unfolds through letters.

feminist criticism   critical approach developed in the 1960s, based on assessing the role of gender in texts. A particular issue is the subordination of women in a patriarchal society.

genre   type of literary work conforming to certain expectations; e.g. tragedy.

Gothic novel   genre of fiction popular in the eighteenth century, in which eerie and supernatural events take place in sinister settings.

idiom   a characteristic expression of a language or **dialect**.

image   a word picture bringing an idea to life by appealing to the senses; a clockwork orange is the central image in the book that carries the name as its title.

industrial novel   dealing with the issues of the Industrial Revolution, often set in the north of England e.g. *North and South* by Elizabeth Gaskell.

irony   a style of writing in which one thing is said and another is meant, used for a variety of effects, such as criticism or ridicule.

magical realism   a fiction style which combines mythical elements, bizarre events and a strong sense of cultural tradition; e.g. *Midnight's Children* by Salman Rushdie.

Marxist criticism   critical approach which sees literature in relation to class struggle, and assesses the way texts present social realities.

metaphor   a compressed **simile** describing something as if it were something else.

narrator   in a novel, a character who tells the story. An *omniscient* narrator has complete knowledge of everything that takes place in the narrative; an *unreliable* narrator is one whose knowledge and judgements are limited and biased.

onomatopoeia   use of words whose sound imitates the thing they describe.

paradox   something that seems nonsense or self-contradictory (but isn't).

parody   an exaggerated copy (especially of a writer's style) made for humorous effect.

persona   an assumed identity.

personification   an **image** speaking of something abstract, such as love, death or sleep, as if it were a person or a god.

picaresque   type of novel popular in the eighteenth century, featuring the adventures of a wandering rogue; e.g. *Tom Jones* by Henry Fielding.

plot   the story; the events that take place and how they are arranged.

polemical   (of style) making an argument.

rhetorical   expressed with a view to persuade (often used in negative sense).

satire   literature which humorously exposes and ridicules vice and folly.

simile an **image** comparing two things similar in some way but different in others, normally using 'like' or 'as'.

standard English the particular form of English, originally based on East Midlands dialect, most often used by educated speakers in formal situations.

stream of consciousness technique exploring the thought processes and unconscious minds of characters; used by writers such as Virginia Woolf and James Joyce.

structure the organization of a text; e.g. narrative, plot, repeated images and symbols.

subplot subsidiary plot coinciding with the main plot and often reflecting aspects of it.

tone the mood created by a writer's choice and organization of words; e.g. persuasive.

viewpoint the way in which a narrator approaches the material and the audience.

NDEX

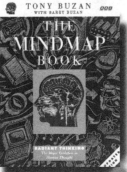

32001